D1481383

Climbing Higher

Overcoming Spiritual Obstacles

DOROTHY DAVIS

REGULAR BAPTIST PRESS
1300 North Meacham Road
Schaumburg, Illinois 60173-4806

Dedication

To Barb Palmiter,
faithful friend and sister climber

CLIMBING HIGHER: OVERCOMING SPIRITUAL OBSTACLES

© 2001

Regular Baptist Press • Schaumburg, Illinois

1-800-727-4440

RBP5252 • ISBN: 0-87227-212-5

Printed in U.S.A.

All rights reserved

Contents

Preface

I love mountains! The White Mountains of New Hampshire, the Berkshires of Massachusetts, the Rockies—American and Canadian—I have seen these and more. I never tire of viewing panoramic scenes from some lofty spot. It refreshes the soul and clears the senses.

The Christian life consists of mountaintop experiences as well as spiritual valleys, with many obstacles in between. To reach the point of some sweet, new view of God's work and character may take great spiritual work on your part. You may get pricked by some briers (those little convictions of the Spirit). You may have to remove some debris (sin) from your path. You will definitely have to expend some spiritual energy (Bible study and prayer) to reach new plateaus. But the view from above is certainly worth it!

The climb to new spiritual heights is a challenging and continual one. Perhaps you've only just begun. Whatever your spiritual status, the enabling power of Jesus Christ is available to see you through every obstacle. Sometimes the going gets rough; sometimes it seems easy. God's Word, the Bible, gives direction for every step. Here we go then. Let's climb together!

How to Use This Study

Each lesson in this study is divided into five sections. Follow these suggestions as you prepare each lesson.

I. PREPARING TO CLIMB

Following the introductory comments, these questions will prepare your heart to study God's Word. The answers to these questions will not be discussed in class.

II. FINDING A FOOTHOLD

The questions in this section concentrate on the actual text of God's Word and will help you understand what God's Word says.

III. PRESSING UPWARD

As you answer the questions in this section, you will see how the truths of God's Word apply to your life.

IV. REACHING NEW HEIGHTS

This section is personal. It is designed as a starting point to help you put God's truth into practice.

V. VIEW FROM THE TOP

These final words will help seal firmly in your mind what you learned from the Bible passage.

Becoming an Overcomer

"For whatsoever is born of God overcometh the world:
and this is the victory that overcometh the world, even
our faith. Who is he that overcometh the world, but he
that believeth that Jesus is the Son of God?" (1 John 5:4, 5).

The Bible, God's written Word, introduces us to the reality of living victoriously in this world. God invites each of us to be an "overcomer," one who has, through Christ, triumphed over Satan, sin, and Hell. The first thing we must do to be overcomers is to receive Christ, to be found in Him.

What satisfaction could a person gain from being a fake? In 1906 a mountain climber named Frederick Cook organized a party of men in an attempt to be the first to conquer Alaska's Mount McKinley. Shortly after arriving and realizing the prospects of success were hopeless, Cook suddenly announced that he would take three of the men and climb the mountain. He returned in less than a month, claiming victory. This was a virtually impossible amount of time for such a climb. However, one of the three men secretly admitted that *he* had never climbed Mount McKinley, and a supposed photo of the same man on top of the mountain was later exposed as a fake! This Doctor Cook, claiming to have reached the summit, hadn't even taken the first step toward climbing it!

Many people today claim to be Christians. They think that being born into a family that practices a certain religion makes them Christians. Or they feel that attending a certain church, being baptized, giving money, or going through a ceremony makes them Christians. They may pretend to be followers of Christ or be quite sincerely ignorant of God's truth.

Nevertheless, these people are fake Christians when measured by the teaching of Scripture. They can't possibly reach the heights of the victorious Christian life, because they haven't even taken the first step: becoming a real Christian. God desires every woman to be an overcomer in this life. Let's examine the first step necessary to such a life.

I. PREPARING TO CLIMB

• Do you know for certain that you will go to Heaven to be with Christ when you die?

• On what do you base this certainty?

II. FINDING A FOOTHOLD

1. A person who is in slavery, blind, lost, and dead is not exactly an overcomer! Yet spiritually, this is how God describes every person who has never made a personal decision to receive Jesus Christ into his or her life. The problem is our sin, which separates us from God, Who is holy. Jot down what each of the following verses tells us about ourselves apart from Christ.

Romans 3:23

Ephesians 4:18

John 8:34

Ephesians 2:1

Isaiah 59:2

2. According to the following verses, unless a person's sins are forgiven, or erased, what will be her eternal destiny?

Romans 6:23

2 Thessalonians 1:7-9

3. Many people today mistakenly think that they will get to Heaven by being good or doing good deeds. But this is *not* what the Bible teaches. Being good cannot erase the sins of sinful people, nor can religious works or ceremonies take away our iniquities. How do the following verses refute the false idea that good works will get us into Heaven?

Romans 3:10-12

Titus 3:5

Matthew 7:21-23

Isaiah 64:6

2 Timothy 1:8, 9

4. God, Who both hates sin but richly loves each sinner, provided a way for us to be forgiven, reconciled to Himself, and made recipients of His gift of eternal life. He sent His Son, the Lord Jesus Christ—Who is Himself God—to die on a cross, bearing God's punishment for our sins. Since He never sinned, He died not for His own sins but for the sins of each person who has ever lived. Summarize the truth about Christ as presented in each of these verses.

John 3:17

1 Corinthians 15:3

1 Peter 3:18

Romans 5:8

5. The Bible declares that Jesus not only died, but that He rose from the dead three days later as proof that He is God and that His death for us was acceptable to the Father. Read these verses. What did His resurrection accomplish?

Romans 1:4

1 Corinthians 15:3-6

1 Peter 1:3

6. A woman can receive forgiveness of sins, eternal life in Heaven, and salvation from God's judgment by receiving Christ as her Savior and putting her faith in His work on the cross as the only payment for her sins. What do the following verses teach you about how a person can

have God's gift of eternal life? For each verse, write down the verb, or action, God requires.

John 1:12

John 6:47

Romans 10:9, 10

Romans 10:13

7. How does the Bible *assure* us that when we repent of our sins and come to Christ, asking forgiveness and inviting Him to come into our lives, He will do as we ask?

John 6:37

John 10:28

1 John 2:25

1 John 5:14, 15

8. In each of these passages, what description is given of the person who has put her faith in Christ?

1 John 5:4, 5

Romans 8:37-39

2 Peter 1:3

III. PRESSING UPWARD

1. God emphatically declares that success, fulfillment, and victory in this life can take place only when a person establishes a right relationship to God. The *only* way we can come to Him is through Jesus Christ's atoning death. Jesus said, "I am the way, the truth, and the life: no man cometh unto the Father, but by me" (John 14:6). Many people go through life trying various means to feel successful. What are some of the ways people endeavor to fill their lives? Why can none of these things *guarantee* success?

2. Some people have just given up hope. For them, perhaps, life has been a series of rejections, disappointments, bad decisions, and failure. Far from being overcomers, they merely exist from day to day. Christ came to lift us from the dust of sin and despair and give us hope and strength. How has Christ brought meaning to your life? Or, to what areas of your life do you want Christ to bring new hope?

3. Many obstacles can prevent a person from putting her faith in Christ. Select three of the following terms and explain how each might possibly hinder a woman from receiving Christ as her Savior. How can God and His Word remove these hindrances?

Pride

Fear

Ignorance

Satan

"Religion" or self-righteousness

Guilt

4. When did you take the first step to becoming an overcomer? What caused you to realize your need for a Savior?

IV. REACHING NEW HEIGHTS

Has God spoken to you through His Word? Spend a few moments in prayer, committing one of the following areas to Him. What *action* can you take to obey God? Allow Him to work in your life as He seeks to make you an overcomer!

_____ I need to receive the Lord Jesus Christ as my Savior. I am now praying this prayer to Him: "Dear Lord, I know that I am a sinner and need to have my sins forgiven. I believe that You sent Your Son, Jesus Christ, to die for my sins and that He rose again and now lives in Heaven. I am asking Him to come into my life and give me Your gift of eternal life. Please forgive me and receive me. Thank You for loving me and answering my prayer."

_____ I am a Christian, but I know that I am not living a victorious spiritual life. I am going to pray that the Lord will teach me His truth through the coming weeks and that I will grow in grace as I study His Word.

_____ I am a believer who is learning much about living for Christ. Right now I am asking God to show me through this study in His Word any areas or attitudes that are not reflecting His glory.

V. VIEW FROM THE TOP

A personal relationship with God through faith in Jesus Christ enables you to be an overcomer in both life now and life after death. Apart from Him, you are lost in your sins and face eternity in Hell, separated forever from God. (This is the clear teaching of Christ Himself in Scripture. Read John 3.)

When we receive God's grace and wondrous gift of eternal life by faith, true satisfaction is just beginning. No, Christ doesn't necessarily change our circumstances, but He can exchange our weakness for His power to live victoriously through them. He doesn't guarantee us riches in material wealth, but we have infinitely valuable spiritual riches and resources. He doesn't always give worldly success and renown, but we can attain spiritual success and receive a rich welcome in Heaven by the Lord Himself.

When we come to Christ, we are "more than conquerors" (Romans 8:37). In Him, we're prepared to scale the heights to spiritual stability. But the first step is crucial, yes, indispensable! Without it, you'll be forever doomed to the "lowlands of despair." Have you taken the first step?

Learning to Climb

*"For the word of God is quick, and powerful, and sharper
than any twoedged sword, piercing even to the dividing
asunder of soul and spirit, and of the joints and marrow,
and is a discerner of the thoughts and intents of the
heart" (Hebrews 4:12).*

Anyone who seriously desires to go on an expedition to the peak of
some great mountain like Everest or McKinley wouldn't equip
herself with sneakers and a bag of potato chips! Committed climbers use
the proper means and materials to assure their ascent. Axes, ropes, tents,
clothing to withstand subzero temperatures, even oxygen tanks, are just a
few of the necessities to ensure success.

If we are serious about the Christian life, devoted disciples of Christ
who grow and mature to spiritual stability, we must avail ourselves of the
means God has provided. He has promised to give us all that we need for
life and godliness (2 Peter 1:3).

Is your spiritual life stale and shriveled? Has it been months, maybe
even years, since you've learned something new and exciting about God?
When was the last time Christ's power did something wonderful in you
or for you? Perhaps you are a new Christian, just starting out, and you
need to know how you can advance spiritually.

You've got some strenuous climbing ahead, but don't be discouraged.
There is a sure means of progress, so put on your hiking boots! If you are
serious about your relationship to God, new heights are just in view.

How often do we eat?

I. PREPARING TO CLIMB

• How often do you

read the Bible on a personal level?	daily	occasionally	seldom
pray?	daily	occasionally	seldom
attend church services/Bible study?	regularly	occasionally	seldom

• Have you—at some point in time after receiving Christ—made the personal decision to totally give your life to God's control? When?

II. FINDING A FOOTHOLD

1. Receiving Christ as Savior is just the beginning of spiritual growth. The Bible uses the term "born again" to describe salvation (John 3:3). Just as a new baby must grow and learn, a new Christian must as well. But for some believers, growth fizzles and stagnation sets in, continuing on for years. If this is true for you, you can begin to find joy and fulfillment in Christ today! How do these verses encourage us that Christ wants to lead us forward to new spiritual growth?

Philippians 1:6   *He will complete the good work He has begun in us.*

Philippians 2:12, 13
Continue to live for him. We are to live our lives so they show what's on the inside.

Philippians 3:12–14
None of us has arrived but we should respond to what He wants us to be.

Colossians 2:6, 7
We accepted Christ by faith, so we grow in Him by faith.

2. If God wants us to grow, then He must provide the way. Although as believers we are God's children, we are helpless to make ourselves "good"; we are totally dependent on His grace and power. What do these verses teach you about the basis for living the Christian life? The first verse presents the problem we face; the others, God's solution.

Romans 7:18, 19 *I need this power of Christ in me to empower me to do what is right.*

2 Corinthians 12:9

My grace is sufficient for thee. His power works best in our weakness.

Galatians 2:20

Christ living His life through me & we live in these earthly bodies by trusting in the Son of God.

Ephesians 6:10, 11

We need to be strong with the Lord's mighty power & put on the whole armor of God.

Titus 2:11, 12

We should turn from godless living & sinful pleasures & live with self-control, right conduct & devotion to God.

1 Peter 5:10

God will perfect, establish, strengthen & settle us after we have suffered a while.

2 Peter 3:18

We are to grow in the grace & knowledge of our Lord Jesus Christ.

2 Peter 1:3, 4

As we know Jesus better, His divine power gives us everything we need for living a godly life. He has called us to receive His own glory & goodness.

3. Living a steadfast Christian life from the New Testament point of view is more than "God helping us." It is God *enabling* us, God working in us and through us. How do the following verses affirm this truth?

John 14:23

God in Christ is living in me

John 14:16, 17 (also 1 Corinthians 6:19)

The Holy Spirit of truth lives in me

4. The Holy Spirit is the Third Person of the triune Godhead. He is fully God, yet He dwells in every believer. According to these verses, how does He work in us to enable us to live the life God desires?

John 14:26

The Holy Spirit will teach & remind us what Jesus taught of the teaching of Christ.

John 16:13

The Holy Spirit speaks of Christ. & He guides us into all truth.

2 Corinthians 3:18

When the Holy Spirit lives in us, He works within us to help us become more like Jesus Christ

Galatians 5:16-25

The Holy Spirit gives us the desires that are opposite from what the sinful nature desires.

Ephesians 3:16

He strengthens us by His Power & gives us inner strength

5. Along with the Spirit, God has given us His Word, the Bible. The Bible is much more than a book; it is the actual written communication of God to us, His very words to the human race. The Word of God possesses the power of God. The Spirit of God uses the Word to change us and guide us. Therefore we must respect it, study it, and obey it. What does the Bible declare about itself?

Psalm 119:89, 160

*Gods word never changes
Gods " is eternal*

2 Timothy 3:16

The scripture makes us wise unto salvation.
To produce faith in Jesus Christ. It teaches right & wrong
Rebukes when wrong
2 Peter 1:20, 21
Corrects me
It is inspired by God & useful to teach us
what is true & makes us realize when we are wrong

6. Why did God give us His Word according to these verses?

John 5:39
The Scriptures point to Christ & in Christ
we have eternal life.

Romans 15:4
The scriptures were given to us to encourage us.

2 Timothy 3:15-17

It gives us the wisdom to receive salvation
& equips us for every good thing God wants
us to do.

1 Peter 2:2
Full growth by reading the Word

Psalm 119:9
Help me from sinning & cleanses our ways

Psalm 119:130
The benefits of the Word of God.
It gives us light & understanding.

7. Prayer is the third resource and privilege God has granted us to aid
in our spiritual maturity. How will praying help us to grow as stated in
these verses?

Hebrews 4:14-16
He is our High Priest. We will receive God's
mercy & grace to help us when we need it.

1 John 5:14, 15
He hears & answers us whenever we ask anything
in line with His will.

Philippians 4:6, 7

Instead of worry – Pray. We will experience God's peace.

Matthew 26:41

Pray that you might not fall into temptation. Be on guard – take responsibility – above all Pray.

8. Another provision of God to assure our continued progress is the church. At the moment we receive Christ, God places us into this "body," which is made up of all true believers (Romans 12:5). Of course, only God can see this entire, worldwide group of people. But in practical, tangible form, God has established local churches, small groups of genuine disciples meant to be our spiritual encouragers. From the following passages, generalize what being part of a local church accomplishes.

Acts 2:41-47

The church teaches doctrine
fellowship
communion
prayer
meeting of ones needs
meeting of needs.

Ephesians 4:11-16

Growth takes place Edification
Each member – serves one another
Building up, unity, maturity

9. God's part has been to provide His children with the resources to enable them to go on in the faith. What, then, is our part? The crucial factor in spiritual growth is the proper attitude toward God and His work in us. What should your mind-set be with regard to your relationship to God?

Hebrews 11:6

Diligently seek Him

Deuteronomy 4:29

Seek Him with your whole heart & soul.

We have a responsibility to grow

2 Timothy 2:15

Study to present ourselves approved to God, being a good worker who does not need to be ashamed.

2 Timothy 2:20, 21

Keep ourselves pure.

2 Peter 3:13, 14

Make every effort to live pure & blameless lives.

God has given us a free will; He wants us, out of love for Him, to totally and unreservedly give ourselves to Him. As you yield control of your whole life into God's hands, you allow Him to be God in your life rather than being your own little god. Only as you completely surrender to Him is He free to work in your life all that He wants to accomplish. Having surrendered to God, you can respond and obey in Christ's power.

10. In your own words, explain how Romans 12:1 and 2 urge you to give yourself totally to God.

Give our bodies to God to live the way He wants us to. Don't copy the behavior & customs of the world, but let God transform us into new people by changing the way we think.

III. PRESSING UPWARD

1. <u>True Christianity is not a religion but a *relationship* with the living Christ,</u> Who desires us to press on to a life of power over sin and fruitful service. For each of the following items, summarize what God has done for your growth and what you must do to grow.

	God's Provision	**My Part**
Holy Spirit (Ephesians 4:30; 5:18)	*He lives within me. Sealed for the day of redemption.*	*not to grieve Him but let Him control my life. Be filled with the Spirit.*
God's Word (2 Timothy 2:15; James 1:22-25)	*is like a mirror to show us what needs to be changed —* *not only a hearer but a doer.*	*Study & obey. Be a doer, not a hearer only.*
Prayer (Ephesians 6:18)	*has great power*	*Pray everyday.*
Local church (Hebrews 10:25)	*helps one grow* *Be at the church — want to help others grow.*	*Be involved in church ministries.*

2. Spiritual progress can be hindered by many obstacles, as we will see in the lessons to come. Name five hindrances to spiritual growth that you have observed in your life.

Lack of discipline
Desire for material things.

3. It may be termed "surrender," "dedication," "commitment." It is not a ceremony or an ecstatic experience, but a deliberate act of the will in which you realize that you need to give God total control of your life. It may be public or private, somewhat emotional or perfectly calm; but God wants you to allow Him to be Lord of your life. Have you ever presented yourself to God in this way? If so, when?

IV. REACHING NEW HEIGHTS

Has God spoken to you through His Word? Spend a few moments in prayer, committing one of the following areas to Him. What *action* can you take to obey Him? Allow Him to work in your life as He enables you to climb!

_____ I want to yield total control of my whole life to God. I recognize that He wants me—my spirit, my mind, my body—to honor and glorify Him. Right now I will pray to Him and present myself as a living sacrifice and will continue to strive to serve Him as I yield to Him anew each day.

_____ I realize that I have been "trying to be a good Christian" in my own strength rather than relying upon God's grace and power and His Holy Spirit's work in me. By faith I look to Christ to live out His resurrection power in me (Galatians 2:20). Daily I will seek to abide in Christ so I can do His will.

_____ I have not been studying God's Word as I should. I am committing myself to spend some time daily learning something new from the Bible. I will ask for the Spirit's help and teaching as I do this. My prayer life needs to be renewed. I am confessing to God my sin of prayerlessness, asking Him to work in me the desire to pray. I will act in obedience by committing some time to prayer with God each day.

_____ I need to become part of a local church. I will seek to join myself to a Christ-exalting, Bible-preaching church and attend services regularly so that I can be taught the Scriptures and be encouraged in the faith.

V. VIEW FROM THE TOP

James 4:8 declares, "Draw nigh to God, and he will draw nigh to you." Have you ever heard the saying, "If you are far from God, guess who moved?" God never forsakes us, but we are always "prone to wander." God is waiting for us to draw nigh to Him, to diligently seek after Him with all our hearts. As we set our wills to do this, He works in us a deeper desire and rewards us with the joy and blessing of a fulfilling spiritual life. Perhaps you have been going through the motions of Christianity. Are you longing to know God and Christ in a real, personal way? New vistas of Their love, grace, joy, and peace are within reach. Draw nigh to God. Begin to climb. He will reach down to you and lift you up.

What can you do today that will show Him the longing of your heart? Do it and trust Him to teach you to climb. You won't be disappointed at what He has ahead for you!

The Perils of Pride

"But he giveth more grace. Wherefore he saith, God resisteth the proud, but giveth grace unto the humble" *(James 4:6).*

Those little yellow signs, "Falling Rock Zone," would strike fear into my heart as a youngster. Driving along curving country roads, I'd look up to see rocks, *lots* of rocks, perched precariously above us as we cheerfully drove along. My active imagination had no difficulty picturing those boulders bouncing down the hill and onto our car! Some comfort the little yellow sign would have been in such a situation!

From a Biblical perspective, pride is the mother of all sins. I am increasingly amazed at the number of disguises in which pride can reveal itself or hide itself, as the case may be. Like those perilous rocks on the hillside, pride is perched in our hearts, waiting to fall upon us from a dozen different directions and in various shapes and sizes. Some of pride's many forms are vanity, conceit, unforgiveness, self-pity, rude behavior, and jealousy.

For a follower of Christ, pride is perilous. It can take root silently and, unless checked, can spread its vicious vines, choking out the spiritual life God desires for us. Not surprisingly, Scripture has much to say about pride. In each lesson of this study, the problem dealt with has its root in pride.

Pray right now that as you study God's Word, the Holy Spirit will reveal to you any areas of pride that are perilous to you.

I. PREPARING TO CLIMB

Think back to yesterday. Was your behavior characterized by any of the following attitudes or actions?

— Became offended because you were not recognized or treated as you wished.

— Boasted about your accomplishments or abilities.

— Reacted defensively or snippy when asked about something you did.

— Became annoyed or angry when asked by an authority figure to do something.

— Bluntly criticized someone for how he or she did something.

— Engaged in a conversation in which you put someone down.

— Used a critical spirit to compare yourself to another person.

— Behaved in a rude, insensitive manner toward someone.

II. FINDING A FOOTHOLD

1. Let's begin by looking at pride in its most defiant form: self-exaltation. This is setting up ourselves as little gods, taking God's rightful place, as we grasp at power to do what we want and to gain honor for our accomplishments. This was the very first sin, initiated by Satan before the world began. Explain how the person (or people) in each of the following passages attempted to exalt self and rob God of His glory.

Isaiah 14:12-15 *Satan wanted to be like God but instead he was cast out of Heaven*

Genesis 3:1-6 *Eve wanted to be wise like God. Satan told Eve to eat of the fruit of the center of the garden or she would die. He tempted Eve by planting thoughts of self-exaltation. "Ye shall be as other Gods."*

Daniel 4:28-37 *Nebuchadnezzar was very conceited he wanted all the glory for himself instead of giving God the glory. His heart was lifted up in pride.*

2. What is God's opinion of self-exaltation according to these verses?

Isaiah 42:8 *God will not give His glory to anyone else nor share with idols.*

Matthew 23:8-12 *He is a jealous God. Only God is our Father. He alone should be given glory. We are to consider God & Christ our Master & we are not to exalt ourselves.*

Rebellion follows closely on the heels of self-exaltation. Exalting of self causes rebellion against God's authority and the authority of those whom God has placed over us. A person who rebels disregards God's Word. A rebel's motto is, "I don't have to!"

3. (a) In Numbers 16:1-3 how did Korah display rebellion? *He incited a group to go against Moses. They told Moses, he acted like he was the only one that God spoke to & they thought he went too far. Korah challenged Moses position & felt that he & others had an equal right to rule.*

(b) With what qualities did Moses respond in verses 4-7? *He challenged them, Moses fell on his face & humbly left his defense in God's hands. God will make the decisions.*

(c) What was God's response to Korah's rebellion in verses 32-35? *The earth opened up & swallowed the whole household. God judged Korah by the first sentence.*

4. What do the following verses teach about rebellion to authority?

1 Samuel 15:22, 23 *Obedience is far better than sacrifice. Rebellion is equal with disobedience to God. Witchcraft, iniquity, idolatry, & rejecting God's Word.*

Romans 13:2 *Those who refuse to obey God will be punished. Rebellion is resisting the ordinance of God.*

when I rebel against authority I am rebelling against God.

The next pride-related sin is self-centeredness. While a believer may never wish to exalt herself above God or rebel against authority, she may regularly place herself in the center of attention—her own and other people's. Self-centeredness is characterized by continually evaluating everyone and everything by how they relate to *me*. When we become obsessed with ourselves, we demand everyone's time, attention, and perfect fulfillment of our expectations. This obsession leads to behavior that is easily offended (irritable, touchy), demanding, hurtful, self-pitying.

5. (a) Read Luke 15:11-32 and explain how both sons displayed self-centered behavior.

The one son was greedy. He wasted his inheritance on self-indulgent living.

The other son was jealous. He was self-centered, resentful & unforgiving. He didn't care for either his father nor his brother.

(b) How is the father's behavior a sharp contrast? *also gentle, patient & compassionate*

He was a loving father & was happy his son came to his senses & was willing to come home & ask for forgiveness.

The last aspect of pride we will deal with in this lesson is <u>faultfinding,</u> or being critical. When we engage in faultfinding, we are often guilty of putting others down to build up ourselves in our own minds. Faultfinding is expressed in various ways: <u>nit-picking, sarcasm, engaging in conversa</u>tions that put others down. It is different from constructive criticism, the aim of which is to help a person without demeaning him or her.

challenge your thinking

The following people exhibited a critical attitude. Read each passage and answer the questions with regard to the faultfinder and the "accused."

6. Eliab versus David: 1 Samuel 17:13-18, 20, 26-29. (a) Of what did Eliab accuse David? *of being proud, naughty & nosey.*

He was David's oldest brother

(b) Was David guilty? *He was not guilty of any of the things Eliab accused him of*

(c) What manner of words did Eliab use? *He put down his youngest brother. Eliab was the oldest son.*

Belittled him & put him down

(d) Why might Eliab have felt compelled to put David down and build himself up? *Perhaps because Eliab was the oldest, his pride in being in Saul's army or his jealousy of David being anointed as king*

Eliab
misjudged
David's heart

(e) What understanding did Eliab lack? Eliab didn't understand that David was obeying his father's instructions & carrying out God's will against the Philistines.

7. The Pharisees versus the blind man: John 9:13-34. (a) Of what did the Pharisees accuse the blind man? They accused the blind man of being an ignorant sinner.

(b) What had the blind man done wrong?
He had done nothing wrong.

(c) What manner of words did they use to attack the man? *harsh*
They used intimidating questions, sarcasm & insults.

(d) Why might they have felt compelled to put him down and build themselves up? They felt proud of their position & probably felt the conviction of sin in their hearts, which caused them to act with malice.

(e) What understanding did they lack?
They lacked understanding about Jesus as God's Messiah. Power does not reside in the man who was healed.

8. The disciples versus the woman: Matthew 26:6-13. (a) Of what did the disciples accuse the woman? They accused her of wasting money & not giving to the poor.

(b) Was she guilty of wrongdoing?
No, she was not doing wrong.

(c) What manner of words did they use in this situation?
They criticized her by murmuring & complaining in a "gossipy" way.

(d) Why might they have felt the need to build themselves up?
Perhaps they wanted to seem superspiritual or were pricked in their hearts by her loving worship of their Master.

(e) What understanding did they lack?
They did not understand the importance of worshiping God's Son, a desire to worship the Lord.

We know that God cannot be pleased with sinful pride. As with any sin, pride must be brought to our awareness by a renewing of our minds through Scripture and the Spirit. Once we are aware, we must repent, ask forgiveness, and yield to God's grace and power to obey in any tempting situation. *See Galatians 6:1*

9. As believers, what transformed attitudes must we develop to counter self-exaltation?

Proverbs 3:5-9 *We must trust totally in the Lord & not in ourselves, acknowledge Him in every area of life & seek His will, fear the Lord & honor Him even with our material possessions.*

Psalm 34:1-3
We must give praise & honor, not to ourselves, but to God.
In all things

1 Corinthians 6:20
We belong to God & are to glorify Him in our bodies & spirit. I am not my own. I am bought with a price.

10. What is God's solution for rebellion to authorities (parents, pastors, government, etc.)? *Practice submission*

Romans 13:1 *Be subject. Be submission to a higher power.*

1 Peter 2:13-17 *We are to submit to them for the Lord's sake. Be accountable to God*

11. The remedy for self-centeredness is humility, the realization of our lowliness and utter dependence upon God. Read Philippians 2:3-11.

(a) List any phrases that help us restrain self-centeredness.
"Let nothing be done through strife or vainglory"
"Esteem others better than ourselves."
"Look not every man on his own things."
Don't be selfish
Don't live to make a good impression on others.
Be humble
Think of others as better than ourselves.
Don't think only of your own affairs but of others also!

(b) How is Christ the model of One Who is *not* self-centered but is completely humble?

As our model of humility, christ made Himself of no reputation, took the place of a servant, humbled Himself to God's will, did not grasp at "rights". He laid aside His glory, & rather than focus on self, He focused on the needs of others. God then exalted Him. How can we put off self-centeredness?

12. Faultfinding, sarcasm, gossip, slander—every hurtful form of verbal put-down is sin. How does Ephesians 4:29 instruct us about these things? (Note that the verse is a command!)

a command   Edifying

mean't grace

That which comes out of our mouths should be good for building up others (not ourselves) & ministering loving kindness to those who hear it. Any not cut down

13. Two parallel passages that have helped me in this matter of pride are James 4:6-10 and 1 Peter 5:5-7. (The key is remembering that we are totally reliant on God's grace to live a godly life!) Look at these two passages and explain what happens when you are proud and what happens when you are humble.

If I react with a proud heart, God will then resist me rather than help me. If I respond humbly (in word, attitude etc.) God will give me grace! When we are proud, God resists you (or opposes you) & when we are humble, He grants grace to help you in that situation.

III. PRESSING UPWARD

Society encourages us in the development and expression of exorbitant pride. "Demand your rights" is now being pushed to the limits of obsession. "Question authority" and "look out for #1" are the catch-phrases of our age. Our thinking about ourselves has been pressed into the mold of the world; it must be transformed by the renewing of our minds by God's Word and His Spirit (Romans 12:1, 2). The world tells us to exalt ourselves; the Bible tells us to abase ourselves.

1. How can you do this and still know that you are a person of worth?

Our sense of worth comes from the understanding that God created us, sought us, redeemed us, loves us, sanctifies us, equips & uses us. Recognise our rightful place under God's power.

2. How might we exhibit an aspect of sinful pride at home or work or church? Select one of the following aspects and record your observations.

Self-exaltation

Rebellion

Self-centeredness

Faultfinding

I have to acknowledge them as sin!

3. What must you do when the Holy Spirit points to thoughts, attitudes, words, or actions of sinful pride? Write your "Bible solution" here. *Repent & confess the sin to God. Ask forgiveness if anyone you have offended. Ask the Lord to point out wrong ideas. Seek to respond humbly in testing situations.*

IV. REACHING NEW HEIGHTS

Has God spoken to you through His Word? Spend a few moments in prayer, committing one of the following areas to Him. What *action* can you take to obey Him? Allow Him to work in your life as He enables you to overcome the perils of pride!

_____ The Lord has convicted me about a problem with self-exaltation. I am confessing this to Him and desiring from this point on to honor Him with my life.

_____ I have been rebellious in my behavior toward (insert name). I am seeking God's forgiveness for this rebellion and choosing to submit to God's will.

_____ The Lord has shown me that my behavior is often rooted in self-centeredness. I am confessing this sin to God and asking Him to develop in me the humility of Christ in my relationships with others.

_____ My speech often betrays a critical attitude toward others. I am confessing this pride to God and asking Him to change my heart and my speech.

V. VIEW FROM THE TOP

The breaking of pride will be a process by which the Spirit convicts us of haughty thoughts, attitudes, words, and actions. We all engage in such behavior from time to time; the goal is to behave so less and less.

Keep a vigilant lookout for pride. Listen for it in your words; see it in your reactions and behavior. Search it out in your thoughts and attitudes. Keep asking yourself, "Why did I say/do/think that?" Continue praying to God about pride: to expose it and extract it whenever it is perched in your heart. God is faithful to reveal pride if we are intent on being free from it. Ask Him to remove the perilous rocks of pride from the hillside of your heart, and replace them with the fragrant, gentle flowers of humility. Ask Him for sensitivity and concern toward the feelings of others as much as toward your own feelings and wants.

Psalm 115:1 declares, as if a prayer, "Not unto us, O LORD, not unto us, but unto thy name give glory." Let us lift up and honor God in all our ways. Sinful pride is not only perilous to us, but it also denies God His position and praise in our lives. The humility of Christ can be ours by continued prayer, confession, and submission, for "God resisteth the proud, but giveth grace unto the humble."

Defenses against Discouragement

*"And the LORD, he it is that doth go before thee; he will be
with thee, he will not fail thee, neither forsake thee: fear
not, neither be dismayed" (Deuteronomy 31:8).*

Recently I heard a news report about some mountain climbers who were halted in their attempt to climb a well-known mountain. A slip of the foot caused an avalanche that swept the climbers down the mountainside, leaving them stranded until help arrived.

Discouragement is most often the result of looking at ourselves in relation to our circumstances. Whenever we take our focus off God and put it on ourselves, we are in spiritual danger. When we "slip" mentally and begin to dwell on how things are not going the way we'd like them to go, we begin to create a threatening wall of emotion that could come crashing down on us. This avalanche of feelings—helplessness, self-pity, apathy, despair—can cause spiritual paralysis that is extremely difficult to overcome.

We all face varying degrees of discouragement, but we don't have to be swept away by it. God's power does not change with our circumstances. We may not be able to change them, and God may choose not to. But we can control our thoughts and find peace in God's providence over all of life.

I. PREPARING TO CLIMB

• How often are you affected by discouragement or self-pity?

____ occasionally   ____ frequently   ____ daily

33

• How do you handle the challenge of these feelings on a spiritual basis?

_____ I tend to become apathetic about God, His Word, and prayer.

_____ I tend to ignore the feelings and continue to have my regular time in God's Word and prayer.

_____ I actively express to God my feelings of discouragement; and, seeking to understand the cause, I study God's Word for a solution and pray about the causes.

II. FINDING A FOOTHOLD

1. Read Numbers 13:17-33 and 14:7. (a) What were the positive factors about the land God had promised the Israelites?

Very good land, Flowing with milk & honey, Bountiful fruit, Very good land

Caleb stood before the Israelites and but the facts before them.

(b) What were the negative factors?

Giants, strong people, walled cities.

1. The facts confirmed.
2. Right attitude - trust in God. We can conquer it.
3. Stated we can conquer it. Believed.

2. What did the ten spies conclude (13:31)?

The Israelites wouldn't be strong enough to go up against the people because of their strength. They would not be able to take the land.

3. What did Joshua and Caleb conclude (13:30; 14:6-8)?

They said they could defeat the people because the Lord would bring them into the land & He would give it to the Israelites.

4. State as many of the causes of the Israelites' discouragement as you can find in the passage.

Fear, feeling of inadequacy, not relying on God, giants were bigger, unbelief

5. To what wrong conclusion about God did their discouragement lead (14:3)?

accusing God of evil

6. List evidences of the Israelites' self-pity (13:33; 14:2, 3).

We are like grasshoppers
" would have been better off dead
" " be better off in Egypt.

7. Why were Joshua and Caleb not discouraged by the same circumstances (14:6-9)?

They were trusting God & believing in His power.

8. To what did the Israelites' discouragement lead? Read Numbers 14:20-35.

Disobedience to God's will, loss of blessing, God's chastening.

9. Although Joshua and Caleb had to suffer loss because of the people's sin, how did God bless them for their faith (14:24, 30)?

They were the only two who were allowed to enter the Land of Promise.

who is your mentor?

10. Read 1 Kings 19. This account of Elijah's discouragement differs somewhat in cause from the passage we've just studied. What were some of the feelings Elijah expressed to God about himself?

He prayed that he might die; he felt he was a failure, he thought his work for the Lord was in vain & he thought he was the only one left. He was overwhelmed by the wickedness of the king, queen & the people.

11. What were some of the likely external causes of Elijah's discouragement?

Jezebel's death threat, weariness, hunger, the evil actions & thoughts of the Israelites.

You don't measure success by nickels & noses.
You do   "   "   "   by

12. The Lord showed gentle compassion in caring for the physical needs behind Elijah's feelings. "The journey is too great for thee" (v. 7) are words that reflect the Lord's understanding of our human limitations. How did the Lord minister to Elijah's physical needs? *He provided food & water & a safe place to rest & sleep.*

13. How did God minister spiritual encouragement and direction to Elijah's heart and mind? *He spoke to him, gave him directions. Told him of the 7000 faithful in Israel. He promised Elisha as a Helper/Companion.*

God never leaves nor forsakes us. God corrected Elijah's thinking.

14. In the following three passages, the persons described could have wallowed in discouragement and self-pity but did not. Select one passage and answer the related questions: (1) Daniel 9:1–23. Daniel had been in captivity, along with his people, for 67 years. (2) 1 Samuel 1. Hannah was barren and harassed by her husband's other wife. (3) Acts 16:16–34. Paul and Silas were in jail for witnessing about Christ.

(a) How did the person or persons respond to the adverse circumstances? *Paul & Silas were in prison & singing hymns to God. Daniel: He read the word of God. He prayed, confessing sin asking God to restore Israel. God sent an angelic messenger to assure Daniel God cares for His people. Hannah: She prayed very honestly & left her cares with God. She left her hands down so to speak. God answered her prayers.*

(b) What did God do to encourage the person or persons? *Paul & Silas: He caused an earthquake to shake the prison, so that the doors were opened & their chains were loosed. Daniel God sent an angelic messenger to assure Daniel of God's sovereign care over His people. Hannah - God answered her prayers.*

15. What verse or passage of Scripture is a source of encouragement to you in trying times?

Psalms 34 + 37 - Isaiah 40
Romans 8:36-39
I Cor. 10:13   Lam. 3:23
Jer. 29:11

III. PRESSING UPWARD

When we are faced with distressing circumstances, we can <u>react or</u> ? <u>respond</u>. (Do you know the difference?) Our thoughts are the key to *Be not* victory or despair. For example, when confronted with a pessimistic *conformed* report about the inhabitants of the land, the Israelites focused on their *to this* own inadequacies and allowed their thinking to become twisted and *world,* idealized (Numbers 14:2, 3). Have you ever reacted to news that way? *but* *Rom. 2:*

1. It is unwise to compare ourselves with others or continually recollect our failures and weaknesses. Explain why such thinking causes discouragement, self-pity, and lack of spiritual progress. *It focuses on* *Galatians 2:20 Ephesians 3:20* *what we are, what God's plan for me is what we should focus on.*

2. Find some verses that address this issue of comparing ourselves with others or succumbing to discouraging thoughts about ourselves. *Gideon* (Use your Bible concordance.) *Exodus 4:10-12 Moses Judges 6:11-16* *Romans 12:3-8 I Cor. 12:13-25 II Cor 10:12* *Do not think more* *Each part of the* *of yourself* *body is necessary* *for each other*

3. What is the difference between examining ourselves and dwelling on our spiritual failures and weaknesses? *Examining ourselves is* *searching our hearts for sins that need to be confessed I Cor. 11:28-31* *to dwell on spiritual failure + weaknesses is wrong because they are not trusting God as their strength*

4. We may sometimes feel inadequate for a task or responsibility we are facing. A current idea we often hear is, "You can do anything you want to do." Why is this a faulty philosophy? As Christians, how might we reword this statement to make it accurate? *It puts the focus on us instead of God's power. God will help me do everything He wants me to do.*

5. Rather than feeling defeated by our insufficiencies, what should we do? What verses of Scripture give instruction in this matter? *Philippians 4:11–13 II Cor. 3:5, 9:8 12:9,10 Look to God for strength & His power for what He wants me to do.*

6. The Israelites began to accuse God of evil intent toward them. How do we sometimes accuse God (by thoughts or words) in times of discouragement? *We think God is unfair.*

7. The Israelites also started to make ridiculous statements like, "We'd be better off back in Egypt." (Read Exodus 1:8-16 and 2:23 to see the faulty reasoning in that statement.) Can you think of ways in which people twist (or idealize) their thinking in times of discouragement? *"Good old days" "If only"*

8. Elijah's bout with defeating feelings indicated some other factors that may contribute to discouragement and self-pity. Consider each of the following areas. How could each contribute to discouragement? How can we minimize the stress of each of these things?

(a) Physical factors, such as weariness and inadequate nutrition (Mark 6:30-32) *Reduce the schedule*

(b) Bombardment of society's wickedness (Psalm 73; Philippians 4:8) *Get into reading the Bible. Focus on kids love, instead of the devils.*

(c) Feelings of isolation (Ecclesiastes 4:9, 10; Hebrews 10:25) *Get into Christian fellowship. Relax*

(d) Overburdened by our tasks (Exodus 18:13-24; Luke 10:38-42) *Set priorities.*

9. In their distressing situations, Daniel, Hannah, and Paul turned their thoughts to God and poured out their hearts in prayer and praise. Their faith in God's deliverance overcame the tendency to become self-pitying and depressed. Do you stop praying when circumstances go sour? Or, when you stop praying, do circumstances "seem" to become sour to you? *Instead I pray more & ask God what I should do about it.*

10. We should go to God with determination and full honesty about how we feel (like Hannah and Daniel did). How will open, honest prayer aid us in working through discouragement? *It helps us focus on God, allows us to express our feelings & concerns to Him & feel His love.*

11. How does praise, not based on how we feel but on the truth of Who God is, help us in these low times? *It focuses on God & know He controls everything.* Prov. 18:2

Fools have no interest in understanding, they only want to air their own opinions.

12. The psalmist said, "It is good for me that I have been afflicted; that I might learn thy statutes" (Psalm 119:71). Why must God's Word become more precious and helpful to us when we don't feel like reading it? *Psalm 40: 2,3 It will provide help & answers for our discouragement.*

IV. REACHING NEW HEIGHTS

Has God spoken to you through His Word? Spend a few moments in prayer, committing one of the following areas to Him. What *action* can you take to obey Him? Allow God to work in your life as He enables you to overcome the effects of discouragement and self-pity.

_____ I often focus on life's circumstances, and this causes me to become discouraged. At such times, I need to reflect on God's power, read His Word, and pray honestly about my feelings, reaching out in faith for God's grace to lift me above the circumstances (Hebrews 4:16).

_____ My discouragement often stems from brooding over failures and inadequacies. I realize that this is an insult to God, Who has created and redeemed me and is able to empower me. I confess this sin and look to Him as my source of enabling.

_____ The Lord has shown me that physical factors are creating discouragement in my life at present. I need to make these changes:

_____ As I encounter discouragement, I want to conquer it by prayer and praise, encouragement from other believers, and meditation on God's character from His Word.

V. VIEW FROM THE TOP

If we "go with our feelings," we will often find ourselves wallowing in wretchedness! To be a spiritual overcomer, we must set our feet on the facts of God's Word. God's presence, God's power, God's protection, His provision—once we place ourselves back on that solid ground, our feelings will follow. Don't be dragged down by discouragement; climb with courage!

L E S S O N 5

The Many Facets of Fear
Part 1

*"There is no fear in love; but perfect love casteth out fear:
because fear hath torment. He that feareth is not made
perfect in love" (1 John 4:18).*

Are you afraid of God? The Bible repeatedly instructs Christians to "fear the Lord." But some Christians are plagued by an alienating fear of God bred from Scriptural ignorance. For many people, it takes years of growth in spiritual understanding to differentiate between the two. As a woman of God, if you are haunted by an unscriptural concept of God, you must recognize it in order to restore a flourishing, intimate relationship with your Heavenly Father.

It seems that fear entered the realm of human emotions as a result of the sin of Adam and Eve in Genesis 3. (This is the point at which Adam and Eve, as individuals and as ancestors of the human race, disobeyed God. Read Genesis 3:10.) This human emotion, when twisted by sin and Satan's lies, results in a mental mess, which must be corrected by a return to Biblical thinking.

All people should have a proper fear of God. The Greek word *phobos* goes beyond the idea of respect to terror. The very being and attributes of God should elicit dread from us as both creatures and sinners. (Why do you suppose Adam and Eve hid after they sinned?) However, as believers in Christ, we no longer need to fear God's *intentions* and *motives* toward us. A careful study of Scripture will clarify this point.

I. PREPARING TO CLIMB

Put a check next to any of the following statements that reflect thoughts you have had.

_____ I just can't please God no matter what I do.

_____ God will punish me for doing/thinking this.

_____ Because I want _____ so much, God will keep it from me.

_____ Things are going all wrong; God must be mad at me.

_____ If I let God control my life, He'll make me be/do what I don't want.

II. FINDING A FOOTHOLD

1. Many people today have no regard for God. They either refuse to believe He exists, or they ignore His being and authority. Read Psalm 2. Summarize its truth about God. What does it state about those who have no regard for God? *God is ruler of the earth, either in reverence now, or in fear judgement later.*

2. Many Bible references tell us to "fear God." This fear is a proper attitude and response based on God's being, His position of supreme authority, and His attributes such as holiness, justice, and power. In each of the following passages, what will a proper fear of God bring about in people's lives?

Luke 12:4, 5 (Christ is speaking)

Fear of God will cause us to turn to God & avoid Hell

Proverbs 8:13

Fear of the Lord causes us to hate evil.

2 Corinthians 5:9-11

A fear of giving an account to Christ how we lived will motivate us to labor faithfully

Hebrews 12:28

Worshipping in the right way.

3. Some Christians imagine God as a mean-spirited tyrant Who is just waiting for them to step out of line so He can zap them with misfortune. Though God does chasten deliberate, continued sin, He does so with loving motives and for our best interests. From each of the following passages, describe God's (or Christ's) qualities toward those who are His.

Exodus 34:6, 7 *merciful, gracious, longsuffering, forgiving.*

Psalm 25:6-10 *Tender in mercies & loving kindness teaching & guiding the meek.*

Psalm 145: 8, 9 *Gracious, full of compassion, slow to anger, shows goodness & mercy to all.*

Hebrews 4:15, 16 *Sympathetic to our struggles, gracious, merciful, willing to help us in our need.*

4. The unbeliever is to fear God's wrath and judgment. The believer is to fear because of her accountability to God, which should bring about holy and disciplined living. But we are not to fear that God's love, mercy, grace, and goodness will fail us when we sin. God sees the intent of our hearts; He knows those who love Him and desire to please Him. What do these verses teach you about fearfulness toward God?

Romans 8:15, 16 *We do not need to be fearful of God, but think of Him as a loving Father.*

1 John 4:16-19 *God perfectly loves us & this removes the fear of being judged if we commit a sin.*

5. One of Satan's schemes is to keep us from trusting God by doubting His goodness. (See Genesis 3:1-6.) After all, if we can't trust God to be good to us, why would we want to give Him complete control over our lives? How does our Heavenly Father reassure us of His good intentions toward us in the following Scriptures?

Psalm 31:19 *Great is His goodness toward those who fear Him.*

East & West — no beginning or ending
north & south. north Pole
South Pole

Psalm 103:1-5 *He provides the following benefits forgives our sins heals our diseases, redeems us, crowns us with lovingkindness*

Romans 8:31-39
God is for us. In Christ, He freely gives us all good things. No one can condemn us & nothing can separate us from his love.

6. You may ask, "But what if I sin? Won't God be angry with me and make something bad happen to me?" Carefully read the following passages and write down what each one teaches you about God's character/ actions/will toward His children.

- Proverbs 3:11, 12
  His character *God loves & delights in us.*

  His actions *He chastens & corrects us when He has to.*

  His will for me *not to despise His chastening nor to detest His correction.*

- Psalm 103:8-14
  His character *He is merciful & gracious, slow to anger, & abounding in mercy.*

  His actions *He has not dealt with us according to our sins, nor punished us for our iniquities*

  His will for me *To fear Him*

- 1 John 1:5—2:1
  His character *God is light & in Him there is no darkness.*

  His actions *Cleanses & forgives our sins & cleanses us from all unrighteousness,*

  His will for me *not to sin but confess it when we do. walk in the light. Fellowship with one another*

Our sins are removed as far as the East is from the West, not north from the South. There is a distinct with Pole + South Pole, but there is no distinct East or West

7. Based on what you have just studied and these additional verses, write a brief answer to each of the following questions. (a) If God does have to discipline us, what is most likely the cause of that discipline (Hebrews 3:12, 13; Proverbs 28:14)? *Discipline will most likely come when we have repeatedly ignored the conviction of His Spirit. + Continuing to sin.*

(b) Is every "bad thing" a chastening from God? (Read John 9:1-3.) *no. Something allow the glory of God to be revealed in the situation. Some things are spiritual tests meant to strengthen us.*

8. As with most spiritual matters, balance is the key. Our understanding of God must be based on Scripture, not too far to the right or the left. God is not our good buddy or a weak, tolerant grandfather. Neither is He a capricious, irritable despot who enjoys watching people squirm and suffer. Explain how the following "pictures" encourage us not to be afraid of God, yet help us still maintain a sense of His transcendence and holiness.

Psalm 23:1-4; Isaiah 40:11 *God is a loving kind shepherd, caring gently for all the needs of His sheep.*

Psalm 91:4 *He is pictured as a mother bird who protects her young ones by covering them with her wings.*

Psalm 103:13, 14 *God is compared to a father who understands his children, their weakness + their limitations.*

Matthew 7:7-11 *God is like a father who would respond kindly to his son. He longs to do good to his children.*

9. The Lord Jesus never excused sin, but He always acted in love and compassion toward every person who understood her needy position before God. Read each of the following accounts and describe the person's need and feelings and Christ's response.

• Luke 8:43-48
Her need *Physical*

Her feelings *She was timid to approach Christ & fearful of His reactions.*

Christ's response
He comforted her, encouraged her & blessed her.

• John 8:3-11

Her need *Spiritual — she needed to be forgiven & to establish a right relationship with God*

Her feelings
Fear & shame.

Christ's response
He forgave her & told her to sin no more.

III. PRESSING UPWARD

Picture the perfect human father. (Of course, no such father really exists on earth.) As you think of this, answer the following questions.

1. What about the father should the child fear? *His position of authority & honor, discipline for disobedience.*

2. What about the father should the child *not* have to fear?
Harm, neglect, rejection.

3. Would a proper fear of the father keep the child from loving her father? Why? *A perfect father would encourage, care, comfort, instruct, meet needs. This would cause the child to love & rely on her father.*

4. Would such a father discipline if

— his child sincerely tried to please him, although the efforts were imperfect? *No*

— his child was too weak, immature, or ignorant to do a certain task? *No*

— his child deliberately and repeatedly disobeyed? *Yes*

5. Why would the father discipline such behavior? *He wants his child to grow up properly & to be healthy.*

6. What kind of discipline would he mete out? *Fair & just & appropriate to the disobedience, breaking the will & not the spirit & leading to the child's repentance.*

7. What would be the nature of the loving relationship between the father and child? *Intimate. They would spend time together & talk. The child would love, respect & trust the father. The father would listen, care, help & encourage.*

8. What goals for the child would guide the father's actions? *For the child to become all the good things she were meant to become.*

9. Perhaps you've guessed by now that the previous questions were meant to bring us to an understanding of our relationship with God. God *is* the perfect Father; we are His precious children. Write a summary of what you have learned about God's attitudes and actions toward you based on your answers to the previous questions. *He loves me & wants what is best for me. He wants me to love & rely on Him. God disciplines me because He wants the very best for me (to become like Christ)*

10. (a) What are some of the reasons a woman might draw away from God in fearfulness? *A poor relationship with her own father, an overly sensitive conscience, ignorance of scriptural view of God, dwelling on her own failures & sins rather than putting them "under the blood by faith", listening to the lies of Satan, comparing self with others.*

(b) How can these causes be corrected?

A deeper knowledge of God through scriptures.

11. The statements in section I reflect wrong thinking on the part of Christians. Here are the statements again. Now explain why we think them and what Scriptural truths we can use to combat these wrong thoughts. Give verses that apply, if you can.

(a) I just can't please God no matter what I do. *Mentally, we overemphasize the verses that reflect God's judgement of sin. We must instead understand His full acceptance of us in Jesus Christ. In these verses we can learn how to please Him. Eph 1:4-6, I Thes. 4:1, Hebrews 13:16, I John 3:22*

(b) God will punish me for doing/thinking this. *With regard to our sinning, we have already seen that God is very merciful & slow to anger in dealing with us. God does not punish us, but He may discipline us if we harden our hearts over a long stretch of continual sinning.*

(c) Because I want _____ so much, God will keep it from me. *God longs to give His children good gifts when they are within His will. Psalms 37:3-5   103:5   Matthew 7:11*

(d) Things are going all wrong; God must be mad at me.

*I John 1:9
Psalms 103: 8-14*

(e) If I let God control my life, He'll make me be/do what I don't want.

Psalms 16:11

IV. REACHING NEW HEIGHTS

Have you fallen into a pattern of wrong thinking about God's motives and intentions toward you? Have you been fearful of God to the point that you have drawn away from a loving, intimate relationship with Him? If so, what reasons might there be for your fearfulness?

Spend some time praying honestly to your Heavenly Father about your thoughts and feelings. Meditate on a verse from this lesson during this week.

V. VIEW FROM THE TOP

All people should reverence and respect God due to His supreme sovereignty. Unbelievers should be afraid because of His wrath and judgment that hangs over them as a result of their unforgiven sin. But believers' sins have been removed through Christ's death; therefore believers should fear God because of all that He is and all He has done. This fear leads to purity of life and fruitfulness of service.

A believer who continually sins and resists the conviction of the Holy Spirit to repent may find herself chastened (disciplined) by some unpleasant experience meant by God to draw her back to Himself. God's goal is for her good and the development of Christlike character in her.

God is very patient and kind toward His children, understanding that in our human flesh we will sin, and giving us grace as we seek to obey Him. A believer never needs to fear God's intentions toward herself. God longs to bless us and do good to us. He desires what is best for us, and we can fully rest in His unfailing love toward us. When troubles come, we should examine our lives for any sin we need to confess or should understand that the test has been sent for our spiritual strengthening.

In our most holy Lord there is much to fear. When the apostle John, in Revelation 1, saw Christ unveiled in all His godly splendor and strength, he fell at Christ's feet as if dead. We are told that this glorious Christ laid His right hand upon John and said, "Fear not." Though able to diminish to dust every person great or small, our loving Lord has stooped to call us His friends and daily embraces us in His most gentle, gracious love.

The Many Facets of Fear
Part 2

"For God hath not given us the spirit of fear; but of power, and of love, and of a sound mind" (2 Timothy 1:7).

Mount Greylock in the Berkshire Mountains is the highest point in Massachusetts. A winding road takes visitors to the top and offers a spectacular view of several states in various directions. On our second visit there, my husband, Dale, and I started the ascent only to find the mountain wrapped in a cloak of thick fog. We continued on to the top, knowing that beyond the fog lay a magnificent vista. But we absolutely couldn't see anything beyond the gray mist that enveloped us on every side.

Fear is an emotion (or perhaps an attitude) that can envelop our hearts and minds, blotting out the clear, majestic view of God's glory. While some fears are healthy, many are not. Certain personality types struggle with fear more than others, but all people fear something.

God understands our tendency to fear; consider how often "fear not" is spoken in the Bible. Fear has many facets, and surely we can't examine them all. Yet because fear can be an obstacle to a full spiritual life with God, we need to penetrate the undetected fog of fear with the truth of God's Word. As our fears roll back, we will see clearly, with eyes of faith, the far-reaching wonder of God's greatness.

I. PREPARING TO CLIMB

List five things that cause you fear. Put a check mark next to the fears that are unhealthy.

II. FINDING A FOOTHOLD

As human beings, we often fear because we can't control. We feel like runners in a race with obstacles suddenly popping up in our path. Life's circumstances can change in an instant; who knows what today will bring? Thankfully, God does, and He *can* control. Each of the following Bible passages gives a cause for fear. Read each passage and answer the questions.

The storm on the lake was a nature kind but there are other kinds of storm in a person's life, causing great anxiety. We have two options to them. We can worry & assume that Jesus no longer cares or by putting our trust in Him. When we feel like panicking confess of your need for God & then trust Him to care for you. We underestimate His power to handle crises in our lives.

1. Mark 4:35–41. Jesus and the disciples were on the Sea of Galilee.
(a) What sudden change in circumstances caused the disciples to fear? *A sudden storm.*

(b) Were these same circumstances troubling to Christ? *Christ was not troubled, He was asleep in the boat.*

(c) What did the disciples have to do to have the circumstances brought under control? *They had to tell Jesus of their need.*

(d) Why did Jesus rebuke them? *He rebuked them for their lack of faith & fear.*

(e) What was the disciples' response to this event? *They had proper fear of Christ as God as opposed to the fearfulness of the storm. I Peter 5:10*

2. Joshua 1:1–11. Joshua and the Israelites are about to enter a new land that God has promised to give them. (a) What attitudes were they to have as they faced these challenges? *They were to be strong & courageous & determined to obey God.*

(b) What actions were they to carry out? They were to do what God commanded, to think on His Words + to prepare to carry out their responsibilities.

(c) What was the assurance God gave them? God's assurance was that He would be with them + not fail them + they would succeed.

3. We have seen from these two passages that, generally, both present circumstances and future unknowns can create fear. Specifically, the many "fear factors" in our lives include loved ones at risk, loss of health, financial stresses, relationship reverses—to name just a few. Yet God is the answer for every fear. What do these verses teach you that will help you put your fears to rest?

Psalm 34:19 *The Lord will deliver me out of all my affliction (as He chooses) We often wish that we could escape trouble, the pain & grief, sorrow, failure etc. God promises to be our source of power, courage, wisdom to help us*

Isaiah 41:10 *I am not to fear, for God will help & uphold me in all circumstances. We need not fear because God's presence is with us. God has established a relationship with us. I'm assured of strength, help + victory over sin; it's continual*

Philippians 4:19 *God shall supply all my needs. but maybe not all in this life, in the new earth when sin has been permanently destroyed, our wants + needs will be supplied for eternity*

1 John 5:14, 15 *God will answer all my prayers within His will. God's will — not mine. When we communicate with God, we don't demand what we want, rather we discuss with Him what He wants for us. If we align our prayers to His will, He will listen & give us a definite answer.*

4. Do you find yourself worrying about what others may think of you? This is a symptom of self-centered pride that can be called the "fear of man." It is a mind-set that puts the opinions of others about us above God's opinion of us. According to Proverbs 29:25, how does this mind-set create a problem in our lives? *It makes it more important to our thinking that it's more important what man thinks of us than what God thinks of us. We aim to please man more than God.*

5. Read 1 Samuel 15:16-24. Explain how the "fear of man" ensnared Saul. Note especially verse 24. *He failed to obey God because he didn't want to displease his people*

(left margin notes) Just as God assured Joshua He would be with him, so He is with us as we face our new challenges. Every day, we face tough, Breaking situations, difficult people & temptations, asking God to direct us, we too can conquer many of life's challenges, obey God's Word, and constantly honor the people of God's truths & daily read & study God's Word. God equals times with obedience

We are more than conquerors

Sometimes He chooses to deliver us from those problems. When trouble strikes we don't get frustrated with God, instead thank Him for being by your side.

Fear of man can hamper everything you try to do. Contrast fear of God. Fear is rooted in reverence + trust is why it is elevating... fear people who do not fear God who turn them into others intended for... onto good who trust the ...

Matthew 10:28

In Gods eyes we faithful work we as for Him has eternal values

6. When we allow our actions to be dictated by the opinions of others rather than the will of God, we put ourselves at risk. How does Psalm 62:5-12 encourage you to put God first? *When we trust God, we remove fear. The opinions of people are vanity. Find something every day to praise God for!! as you do you will find your heart elevated from daily distractions to lasting confidence.*

Another facet of fear concerns ourselves. In this case, a focus on our personal inadequacies creates a hindrance to obeying and serving God because we are afraid to fail. (Do you remember that we studied how the Israelites refused to enter the Promised Land when they focused on their own weakness?) From each of the following accounts, explain the person's fears about himself and God's solution to those fears.

7. Exodus 4:10-12: Moses' response to being sent to Pharaoh.
   Moses' fear – *Moses was eloquent, but slow of speech*

   God's solution – *God who made Moses tongue would enable to say what was necessary.*

8. Judges 6:11-16: Gideon's response to God's assignment.
   Gideon's fear – *Gideon was a nobody (He had no credentials.*

   God's solution – *In Gods eyes, Gideon was a man of valor. and He would be with him (God never deemed credentials)*

9. 1 Corinthians 2:1-5: Paul's testimony.
   Paul's fear – *Pauls human weakness to do God's work in his own power.*

   God's solution – *Preach the gospel (God's Word has power) & be filled with the (Spirits Power)*

10. Fear has some other family members with whom you might be acquainted, namely worry, anxiety, and depression, among others. What does God want us to do about these relatives of fear?

Matthew 6:31-34 *Seek God first, trust Him for our needs. Don't worry.*

Philippians 4:6-8 *Pray - Present our requests with thanksgiving. Let God's peace rule our minds as we focus on thinking right.*

I Peter 5:7 *Cast our cares on God.*

Isaiah 26:3 *Keep our thoughts on God.*

Psalm 42:5-8 - *Hope in God, remember God, trust in His lovingkindness, & His answering prayer.*

11. Two sisters in Scripture, Mary and Martha, illustrate the contrast between the worrisome woman and the peace-filled woman. Read Luke 10:38-42. *Just like Martha, I'm glad Jesus is consistently patient with me!*

Worship begins with silence & listening

• Martha

(a) Describe her attitudes/actions. *In attitude she was stressed out. In action she was frantically busy.*

(b) What was she worried about? *She was worried about her household & supper chores.*

(c) What was causing her fear? *She was fearful that everything wouldn't get done & done to perfection (Pride)*

(d) What did her fear cause in her words and actions? *Her fear caused self-pity & criticism against Jesus & Mary.*

(e) Would you have felt as she did?

• Mary
(a) Describe her attitudes/actions. *She desired to hear God's Word. Her actions were quiet & calm.*

(b) Was she worthy of criticism? *Though it could appear that she was lazy or thoughtless, she was simply putting spiritual matters before food.*

(c) What caused her actions? *Her actions were caused for a deep reverence & love for Christ & a spiritual hunger in her soul.*

• Jesus

(a) What did He say about Martha? *He rebuked Martha for being burdened, worried & troubled.*

(b) What did He say about Mary? *He commended Mary for making a choice for that which was useful & beneficial.*

(c) Why do you think He rebuked Martha? *He rebuked Martha because she chose to be controlled by her feeling of worry regarding material things.*

(d) Why do you think He commended Mary? *He commended Mary because of her spiritual priority. The Lord would have been content to have left them spending quality time with Mary & Martha.*

12. God has given us the spiritual resources to deal with our fears (2 Peter 1:3). According to our memory verse, 2 Timothy 1:7, what has God given us to overcome fear, and how can these things help us? *God's power which can work in any situation is also working in us, love that keeps on loving others in any circumstance, self control to think right thoughts when tempted to fear.*

III. PRESSING UPWARD

1. The disciples in the little boat had sense enough, at least, to turn to the Savior in their time of distress. But what about us? To whom or what might we turn in dealing with our fear? List several examples. *We may turn to other people. Do activities to mask our fears (eating - get fatter, shopping - spend more money, lottery - gambling, watch Television - couch potato).*

2. How would the Lord have us respond in times of fear? _Lean on Him_
Pray honestly.
Read the Word
Keep our mind on Him
ask others to pray

3. (a) Why is it important to deal with our fear? _Fear can get our_
mind off of God & out of God's will

(b) To what sins may fear lead? _Fear can lead to_
disobedience, lying, cheating, jealousy, anger,
hatred, depression.

(c) How can fear affect us physically? _It can make us_
sick — High Blood Pressure
Stomach Problems
Lack of Sleep

4. Can you recall a time when someone's opinion or words caused you to step out of God's will for you? How did you feel afterwards? Did you resolve the problem? How?

5. Moses was tongue-tied—or so he said. Gideon felt like a nobody. Even the mighty apostle Paul, in his human strength, felt shaky and weak-kneed! List some other fears that people have about themselves that, when focused upon, keep them from serving God.
not enough schooling
Shy   _can't do it good enough_
Too old   _It's time for younger folks to_
                take over.

6. How could such fears actually cause us to disobey God's will? How do they cause us to miss out on blessings?
We lose the joy of serving

7. On what must we focus when we feel inadequate to serve God? Can you think of verses that give assurance of God's help? *We must focus on God's power as our source of strength. Philippians 4:13 I Cor. 9:8 12: 9, 10*

8. Debilitating fear and worry are a result of unbelief, and unbelief is sin! When fear overtakes you, what must you do to secure your continued fellowship with Christ? *Confess your sin*

9. <u>Martha, the frazzled worrywart.</u> Mary, the calm, focused worshiper. What is "encumbering" your life right now? How is it affecting your attitudes, words, and actions? your spiritual life? What does Christ want you to do about it? *Trust Him as His way is perfect. Don't worry about tomorrow.*

IV. REACHING NEW HEIGHTS

Has God spoken to you through His Word? Spend a few moments in prayer, committing one of the following areas to Him. What *action* can you take to obey Him? Allow Him to work in your life as He enables you to overcome your fears.

_____ I have been overtaken by fears in my present circumstances. The cause of this fear is _____ . I am claiming the promise of God for help and strength and will pray when fear settles upon me in this matter.

_____ I am fearful of the future regarding _____ . When I am afraid, I will trust in God's promise to be with me and will seek to discern God's will in my decisions.

_____ I often worry about what others may think of me, and this, at times, affects my behavior and decisions. I am asking the Lord to remove this fear and renew my thinking to be ruled by His Word and will.

_____ I have held back from totally serving God because I fear my own inabilities. With God's grace, I am committing myself to step out in faith and yield myself as a servant to God as He burdens my heart to serve Him.

_____ Martha or Mary? The Lord has convicted me that worry and preoccupation with life's demands have caused me to neglect the joy of Christ. I am asking Him to help me slow down, simplify, and take time daily to visit with Him in His Word and in prayer.

V. VIEW FROM THE TOP

Fending off fear doesn't involve a one-time prayer. Like the matter of forgiveness, prayer will be necessary every time wrong thoughts take control of the mind. God's promises and power must conquer fear as you and I meditate on God's character and Word. The Holy Spirit has a part in filling us with peace as well.

If fear of other people's opinions has been influencing your attitudes, words, and actions, confess this to God. Focus on His will for you in His Word. You'll never go wrong if you're right in God's opinion!

Perhaps you've refused to serve God because you fear you're incapable. Oh, how capable God is to work in you and through you! Speaking personally—though I have found the Lord to be very patient in dealing with my timid personality—I have had to step out in faith and obey God's directives, no matter how unsure I felt. And He has been faithful.

Fears? Yes, there will be many fearful moments in life. But as the psalmist declared in Psalm 34:4, "I sought the LORD, and he heard me, and delivered me from all my fears."

Killing the Root of Bitterness

"Looking diligently lest any man fail of the grace of God; lest any root of bitterness springing up trouble you, and thereby many be defiled" (Hebrews 12:15).

A massive pine tree was being removed in our backyard. Right beside it was a great orange blossom bush, well-contented with its position in life. The top of the old pine was quickly taken down, but the extensive root system was a more difficult task. Finally the roots of the pine were extracted, but as a result of the process, very little of the orange blossom bush remained. It was little more than some bedraggled stems sticking out of the ground. I was pessimistic about the fate of that bush at the time, but my fears were unfounded. The orange blossom quickly recovered its vigor and fullness the following season. Its roots had not been touched, allowing those wild, entwining branches to grow heartily again. The pine tree, however, has never reappeared. The total removal of the roots assured that.

The Bible talks about the "root of bitterness." It is a root that, once secure, will resist all efforts to extract it. But what grows from such a root? It is NOT a lovely, fragrant life, as we shall see in our study of God's Word.

I. PREPARING TO CLIMB

Is there a past event in your life that causes you anger, self-pity, depression?

59

Is there a situation that you relive in your mind, rehashing the same old emotions as you dwell upon it?

Is there a person whom you delight to dislike, criticize, mistreat?

Is there a person who looms steadily in your thoughts as the cause of unhappiness or trouble in your life?

II. FINDING A FOOTHOLD

First of all, we must define the word "bitterness." Bitterness is the state of continuing anger and resentment toward a person or situation. It is anger that has been "bottled up" and not dealt with God's way. Let's begin by understanding God's directives about bitterness. Read the following passages and answer the questions.

1. Ephesians 4:30—5:2. (a) What are we to do with bitterness (v. 31)?

We are to put all bitterness away from us. They should have no place in our Christian life.

(b) What results when we do not do as God commands regarding bitterness (v. 30)? *We grieve the Holy Spirit because of our sin. Bitterness builds up & could result in more sin. It can Satan a foothold.*

(c) What attitudes/actions will be involved in "putting away" bitterness (v. 32)? *Kindness, tenderheartedness, a forgiving spirit. Put off bitterness & replace it with kindness & compassion.*

(d) What is the motivation (4:32; 5:1, 2)? *The motivation is Christ's forgiveness of sin, His willingness to love us when we had sinned against Him & our goal to be like Him.*

Read v. 31 — are these sins related?

2. James 3:13-18. (a) In this passage "bitterness" is paired with two other words (v. 14). List them. *Envy & strife. jealousy selfishness ambition*

Bitter envy is jealousy of another's goodness

Don't be a cloud when you can be a star

(b) If we do have bitterness, what two things must we not do (v. 14)? *We are not to boast about it. We are not to lie about it. (How might a person do this?)*

Don't fan the flames & getting it to start again.

Foolishness leads to dis-order, but wisdom leads to peace & goodness.

when our speech is motivated by Satan it is full of jealousy, evil, selfishness, disorder, earthly desire & unspiritual thoughts.

when motivated by God — it is full of mercy, love for others, peace, courtesy, yielding to others, sincerity, goodness, & quiet gentleness.

(c) How is this behavior described (v. 15)? *This behavior is described as earthly, carnal & devilish.*

It's unspiritual & of the devil

Disordered sinful Practice

(d) What does it produce (v. 16)? *It produces confusion & every evil work. (How does this effect the local church?) It causes disorder in the church.*

3. Hebrews 12:14-17. (a) What two problems will the root of bitterness cause for a believer (v. 15)? State what they mean. *It troubles & defiles a person. When a woman is bitter, her mind is controlled by the person or event that caused the anger. She then has no emotional peace. Lack of peace & defiles oneself. Sin always blocks our vision of God so if we want to see God, we must remove it from our lives.*

jealousy dissension & immorality

(b) In verses 14 and 15 we are told to do two things that will keep us from bitterness. What are they? *Follow peace & holiness & watch diligently to keep ourselves in the peace of God. How do we do this? We must pursue peace. Live in peace with all men. Be ye holy as I am holy.*

4. Bitterness is really a matter of unforgiveness, holding a grudge against someone for an injustice, real or imagined. Select ONE of the following passages and explain how the person or persons described became bitter. To what did his or her bitterness lead? *Jacob craftily obtained*

Genesis 25:28-34; 27:6-45 *Esau's birthright. Then Esau's bitterness wanted to kill his brother. Esau traded the lasting benefits of his birthright for the immediate pleasure of food. As we grow in the Lord we have more responsibility. Jacob had the strife.*

Jezebel & Naboth I Kings 21:1-17

Genesis 37:3-28 - *Joseph's brothers became bitter because of their father's partiality & Joseph's egotistical dreams. The brothers sold him into slavery as a youngster Joseph was over-confident & also his father's favorite son. He had a lot to learn & God was teaching him perhaps with some hard lessons. I, too, have had to learn the hard way in my life.*

Esther 3:1-6; 5:9-14 *Haman became bitter because Mordecai wouldn't bow down to him & honor him so He plotted to kill him. But the plot led to his own death. Mordecai's anger was not just toward Mordecai, but toward what he stood for. — the Jews dedication to God as the only authority worthy of reverence. It was prejudice which grew out of personal pride & the only way for him to fulfill these desires was to kill those*

5. In contrast to the persons above, we have the blessed example of Joseph. Sold into slavery by his brothers, put unjustly into prison, then finally promoted to Egypt's second in command, he displayed the attitude of one who truly trusts in God. Read Genesis 45:1-8. How was Joseph's response different from the one about which you just read? (See also Genesis 50:14-21.) *Joseph saw God's hand in the situation. God worked out the situation to produce ultimate good, & Joseph forgave his brothers. He was God's tool. God sent Joseph ahead to preserve lives, save Egypt & to prepare the way for the beginning of Israel.*

[margin note: God's ultimate plan was being fulfilled through the brother's actions]

6. It may be as simple as a hurtful comment or as serious as betrayal, abuse, or abandonment. Whatever the source of our bitterness, the cause is always hanging on to the offense and refusing to forgive the offender. We consider ourselves justified in our continuing anger and have, perhaps, a sense of enjoyment in the resentment we feel. But what does God say about this matter of forgiveness in the following verses?

Luke 17:3, 4 *We must forgive as many times as necessary.*

Colossians 3:12-14 *We are to be forbearing & forgiving even as Christ was. Put off the anger & put on love, gentleness etc. because of Christ*

7. What further instruction does God give us in these verses?

[margin note: Control your thinking]

Leviticus 19:18 – *Do not hold a grudge or seek revenge, but instead love others as yourself.*

Proverbs 20:22 – *Don't repay evil for evil wait upon the Lord to take care of the situation. Don't say I'll pay you back but wait upon the Lord.*

Matthew 5:44-46 – *We are to love, bless, do good to & pray for those who have treated us poorly. (Must we forgive if the person does not repent of the wrong done to us?) If they don't repent, what about our anger?*

Pray & do good to those who despitefully use you.

8. In our bitterness, we may even be angry with God for what has occurred in our lives. God is not the author of sin and evil, but man, in exercising the free will God has given him, may choose to do evil to others. When we forgive and let go of the offense done to us, what can God do in our lives?

Romans 8:28 *God will use all things in our lives to produce good for us.*

Psalm 37:1-9 *When we commit ourselves to God, He will establish & bless us.*

Put off & Put on — Do good — Do right
fretting   Trusting the Lord — Trust in the Lord — Feel right
& do good   and dwelling — safe pasture

If we refuse to let go of our anger and bitterness, great are the consequences: emotionally, physically, and spiritually! In fact the Greek word *pikria*, as in Hebrews 12:15, carries with it the idea of poison. Yes, bitterness is a poison that slowly contaminates and kills the inner life.

9. Read Psalm 73 and answer the questions. (a) What caused the heart of the psalmist to be bitter (vv. 3-16)? *He was envious of the prosperity of the wicked. (Their time is coming) Remember Terry Powells sermon the night Pastor talked with the people who were to be baptized.*

(b) What were the effects of his bitterness (vv. 2, 13-16)? *It caused deep pain, spiritual decline, & a feeling that his obedience to God was in vain.*

(c) What understanding and change of attitudes delivered him (vv. 17-28)? *He was delivered from his bitterness as he focused his thoughts on God's sovereignty & justice.*

III. PRESSING UPWARD

1. Romans 8:6 says that a spiritually minded person has life and peace. What are some of the signs of bitterness in a person's life? *Touchy, anger, sarcasm complaining. a critical attitude, depression, self pity, restless activity. Easily provoked, chip on the shoulder.*

2. God tells us we must forgive. What are some sinful attitudes that keep us from forgiving? _Pride, revenge, desire to control, stubbornness,_

3. Explain why we must forgive others "for Christ's sake," See Ephesians 4:32—5:2 and 1 Peter 1:14-19. _We are to forgive as God has forgiven us. Our lives are to be characterized by love & holiness. God will judge us on how we lived as believers. Christ bought us with His own blood. & we are not free to do as we please, but we are to please Him. He commanded us to. II Cor. 5:9 (look it up) Forgive as God forgave you. Christ as an example_

4. Forgiveness is not a matter of feelings; it is God's supernatural grace enabling us to leave the offense with Him. When feelings of anger return to tempt us, we will need to go to God and claim again His grace and strength. What Scripture verses can you look to at times when you feel you can't forgive? _Ephesians 4:32   Philippians 4:13 — I can do all things through Christ. II Timothy 2:24   Matthew 5:44 - Love your enemies, whether I feel like it or not, I want to lash out._

5. Under what conditions should you go and talk to someone who has offended you? See, for example, Matthew 18:15-17. In what cases might it be better to keep the matter between you and God? _If a person is a believer, he can possibly be confronted about it. Sometimes it's better to keep your mouth shut & take the problem to God & let Him give you peace about the situation._

6. In summary of our lesson, formulate a spiritual plan for the removal of bitterness.

(a) _Be diligent & watch for any bitterness   Heb 12:15   Be alert for symptoms_

(b) _If an offense occurs, forgive, based on God's command in Scripture Matthew 6:14, 15   Forgive immediately_

James 1: wisdom & generously.

(c) *Confess any wrong reactions: pride, wrong words etc.*   *I John 1:9*
Confess it as sin

(d) *Talk to the offender* *Matthew 18:15*
if necessary

(e) *If feelings of resentment occur take them to God in prayer, tell Him all about it & be filled with the Spirit.*
James 4:7, Phil. 4:8, Galatians 5:16
If peace comes it is from God. Do what is good
An idle mind is the devils workshop.

IV. REACHING NEW HEIGHTS

Has God spoken to you through His Word? Spend a few moments in prayer, committing one of the following areas to Him. What *action* can you take to obey Him? Allow Him to work in your life as He enables you to extract the root of bitterness.

_____ I have been bitter about a situation in my life. Perhaps I am even angry with God for allowing it to happen. I now realize that God is not the cause of evil, but that if I submit myself to Him, He can use even that for my good. I am confessing my anger, leaving the hurt in His hands, and drawing near to my Heavenly Father to heal the wound. I am trusting in the love and grace He has for me.

_____ I have been bitter toward (person's name). I recognize that my unforgiveness is sin. I need to forgive him or her just as God forgave me in Christ. I see that, along with disobedience to the Lord, my bitterness has been destroying my life and peace like a poison. I am now confessing my sin to God and am committing myself to forgive whenever thoughts and feelings about this anger reoccur. If necessary, I will go and talk to this person about the offense as well.

V. VIEW FROM THE TOP

When we choose to be bitter, it is not the person or situation that is damaging us; we are damaging ourselves. First of all, bitterness is a poison that chokes out our relationship with God, a form of pride that cuts off His grace (James 4:6). Bitterness becomes the taproot, and branching from it are all manner of other sins such as stubbornness, disobedience, unforgiveness, gossip, and so on.

Secondly, bitterness is a poison that robs us of mental and emotional life and peace. Our minds will continually go back to the offense done to us instead of focusing on what God is doing now. Instead of peace, we have anger, self-pity, critical attitudes. Think again of the story of Joseph. In all his troubles he had the peace of God, but his brothers, though "free" to go where they wanted, lived with guilt and fear. God's way of dealing with life is always best!

Thirdly, bitterness is a poison that can cause physical ailments as well as depression. On top of all this, our bitterness will affect the other people in our lives as they must continually cope with our emotions, attitudes, and physical distress. Bitterness is a selfish sin.

Come to the cross of Christ and leave there the offense and the pleasure of your anger. They have cost you a great deal. The root of bitterness strangles. The Christ Who forgave can enable you to forgive and make you free—free to draw close to your Heavenly Father and free to find Christ's joy and peace.

The Spiritual Significance of Gratitude

"As ye have therefore received Christ Jesus the Lord, so walk ye in him: rooted and built up in him, and stablished in the faith, as ye have been taught, abounding therein with thanksgiving" (Colossians 2:6, 7).

Have you ever stood before the window of a hospital nursery at feeding time? As those tiny tummies send out their distress signals, a clamor of infant sirens arises: pitiful whines, complaining cries, angry screams. Nurses scurry to take the grumblers to the only source of satisfaction—Mother!

We can smile at babies who cry to be fed. They have a need, and they want it met—now! But adults who whine, complain, or scream aren't quite so humorous. Yet, if we're honest enough to admit it, we often want things *now*. In fact, we usually want many things, many times a day, *now!*

But that's the way we are, we reason. People are all a little selfish, a little unthankful, a little impatient. It's not a big deal, spiritually speaking. Or is it?

Gratitude is a key element to spiritual growth. That's a blunt statement, but by the end of this lesson, you'll more fully understand why it's true.

I. PREPARING TO CLIMB

Is thanksgiving a routine part of your prayers to God? *More than requests*

Are you waiting upon God right now for something you want to happen? *yes*

Are you waiting patiently or <u>impatiently</u>?

II. FINDING A FOOTHOLD

Being thankful is no small thing. I'm learning that it is a powerful hinge upon which my spiritual life turns. Gratitude keeps me looking at God, depending on Him. Ingratitude causes . . . well, let's see what ingratitude leads to.

1. Read Romans 1:18-32. This dismal picture maps the downfall of the human race and pictures the potential spiritual condition of every *ungrateful* unbelieving sinner. But look at verse 21. What two attitudes mark the beginning of spiritual downslide? *not being thankful & not honoring God. They wouldn't even admit that they knew God & wouldn't thank Him for their daily care & wouldn't honor Him.*

2. To what immediate spiritual consequences will these two attitudes lead (vv. 21-23)? *Wrong thinking & loose morals. Worshipping other things & not God. Wrong goals. Worshipped idols. gradually one step at a time they went deeper into sin.*

3. Being unthankful leads to discontentment. We stop counting our blessings and begin counting someone else's. Suddenly *we* come up short! We see so much that we don't have, and we begin to concentrate on what we lack. What observation about mankind is expressed in Ecclesiastes 5:10 and 6:7? *Man's desire is never satisfied. Seeking after vain things. The foolishness of thinking that wealth brings happiness. mankind is always looking for something better. Deceitful desires. Eccl 12:13-14 for God will bring every work into judgement including every secret thing whether good or bad.*

4. To what does discontentment lead in James 4:1-3?

tongodly attitude + wrong thinking + praying. It leads to quarrels + we want more of everything + we come greedy.

5. What are we told about contentment in the following verses?
   Proverbs 15:16 *Better with a little with love for God than great treasure without Him*

   Proverbs 16:8
   a little gained honestly is better than wealth if gained by dishonest means.

   Philippians 4:11-13
   Be content in every situation. The secret was Christ power in His life. He will supply all your needs

   1 Timothy 6:6-8
   money doesn't bring happiness. Be content in whatever state you are. Love people more than money.

   Hebrews 13:5
   Be content in everything. God will never leave you or forsake you. He takes care of the lilies doesn't he? Keep your lives are you ever discontented with God

my goal should be godliness. Everything can be taken from us but we will always have God

Some time ago, I discovered that, like many people, I was afflicted with the "if-only" syndrome. In my life, it went like this: If only I were married, I would be really happy; (after marriage) if only I had children, I'd be really happy; (after three children) if only I had a home, I could be really happy; (after buying a home) if only I could fix up this home the way I want it—. Suddenly I recognized in myself this futile pattern of thinking. I realized that while all of these things were good, none was able to completely satisfy my heart and bring contentment. God alone could do that. *the idol of the heart*

A danger with the if-only syndrome is that a person will become so *bent on* obsessed by what she wants, that she will manipulate to get it. (I am *geometry* defining manipulation as "human beings taking action to speed up or arrange circumstances to effect a certain outcome that is contrary to the timing and purposes of God.") Willful manipulation can lead us into dreadful sin and grievous consequences.

6. Select one of the following passages and explain (a) how the person(s) was (were) discontent; (b) how the person(s) manipulated; (c) what sin resulted; and (d) what consequences were suffered.

Genesis 15:1-4; 16:1-6; 21:1-11 *Abram & Sarai*
They couldn't wait for God's leading so they planned to produce a child through the hand-maid

1 Samuel 8:4-22
Israelites demanded a king
Saul's Problems later.

1 Kings 21:1-21 *Nahab & his vineyard*
Jezebel had him slain

Discontentment

7. Unthankfulness may cause us to become impatient with God. We doubt God's goodness, love, power, or willingness to answer our prayers. In the following verses what instruction is given regarding our attitudes and actions as we wait for God to answer our prayers?

Psalm 37:3-7 *Delight ourselves in the Lord*

Psalm 62:5 *wait upon God*

Psalm 130:5
Wait & put hope in His Word

8. (a) Name some people in the Bible who waited patiently for God to work out His plan in their lives. *Hannah, Abraham, David, Job, Daniel, Joseph, Mary*

waited for end to lead him to the land of promise

He did't kill King Saul

(b) What evidence do we have that they had thankful attitudes in their hearts? *Abraham offered sacrifice, while the others gave thanks to God verbally*

9. Read Luke 17:11-19. (a) What does this incident teach us about human nature? *To be selfish & unthankful.*

(b) How was the Samaritan different?
He worshipped & thanked God.

10. When we are spiritually grounded in God and continually grateful to Him for His grace and goodness, these characteristics will be reflected in our lives. Look up these verses and explain how they relate to gratitude in our lives.

1 Chronicles 16:29 *When we are grateful we will give glory to God*

Psalm 5:11 *We will rejoice & be glad*

Psalm 104:33, 34 *We will sing unto the Lord*

Hebrews 13:15 *We will praise God & give thanks.*

11. I stated earlier that gratitude is a key element to spiritual growth. Consider the following passages from Colossians and explain how they support this statement in view of Paul's goals for the believers.

Colossians 1:9-12 *He prayed that the Colossians would give thanks to God*

Colossians 2:6, 7 *They were to abound in thanksgiving*

Colossians 3:15-17 *allow the Word to dwell in us. be thankful.*

Colossians 4:2 *As we pray we should express our thanksgiving.*

12. According to Ephesians 5:18-20, what does giving thanks indicate? *Giving thanks is an indication of a Spirit-filled life.*

III. PRESSING UPWARD

1. Explain why thankfulness is so vitally linked to our spiritual growth. *Within focus on God*

2. What are some symptoms of ingratitude in a person's life? *We become disgruntled complaining*

3. What are some of the if-only wishes upon which people put their expectations for happiness? How do we know that these things can never bring true personal satisfaction?

4. What might be some of the reasons that God makes us wait rather than answering our prayers immediately? Can you think of Scripture verses that support your answers? *Patience & Dependence*

To test our obedience Wrong attitude
strengthen our faith To gratify sinful motives
Perhaps He is working in someone else's life to
answer our prayers.

5. (a) What, then, are we doing when we step ahead of God's plan and try to bring about our desires?

II Cor. 12:9-10
I Pet. 5:10

(b) How does this affect our gratitude?

(c) What are the benefits of waiting for God?

6. What things in your life cause you to be discontent?

7. What kind of thoughts and attitudes does your discontentment stir up? To what kind of words does it lead? to what kind of behavior?

8. What kind of thoughts can you substitute for the if-only thoughts you think?

9. How can we cultivate an attitude of gratitude in our lives?

10. What are the benefits of a life of gratitude?

IV. REACHING NEW HEIGHTS

Has God spoken to you through His Word? Spend a few moments in prayer, committing one of the following areas to Him. What *action* can you take to obey Him? Allow Him to fill your heart with joy as you overcome ingratitude.

_____ I have been whiny, complaining, and critical about aspects of my life. I am confessing my sin to God and seeking to be filled with the Holy Spirit, Who will fill me with joy and praise.

_____ I am suffering from the if-only syndrome. I have been discontent about this matter:_____ . I am confessing this to God, along with any manipulating I have done. I want to trust God's will and timing and wait patiently for Him.

_____ I desire to praise and thank God more. To cultivate gratitude, I will take the following action: _____ .

V. VIEW FROM THE TOP

If you have any doubt about the place of gratitude in the believer's life, simply take a concordance and look up words such as "thanks," "praise," and "rejoice." God's Word is filled with expressions of praise as well as commands to be grateful. Gratitude must be more significant than we realize.

Lack of thankfulness can give rise to discontentment. Discontentment breeds wrong thinking (if only!). Wrong thinking solidifies into bad attitudes (anger, self-pity, criticism), unedifying speech (grumbling, yelling), and ungodly behavior (manipulation, and, if unchecked, moral failure). We have spiraled away from God!

My sister, you and I must count our blessings every day. Yes, life is often difficult, but we have this assurance: "It is of the LORD's mercies that we are not consumed, because his compassions fail not. They are new every morning: great is thy faithfulness. The LORD is my portion, saith my soul; therefore will I hope in him. The LORD is good unto them that wait for him, to the soul that seeketh him" (Lamentations 3:22-25). Now that's something for which we can all be grateful!

The Pull of Worldliness

"Love not the world, neither the things that are in the world. If any man love the world, the love of the Father is not in him" (1 John 2:15).

When a blizzard descends upon a mountain, there is slim hope for the chance traveler upon its trails. One can read accounts of people who perished just yards from a safe shelter because they could not get their bearings in the onslaught of blinding snow. Often victims will just lie down peacefully and succumb to the cold!

Like a furious blizzard, a barrage of worldly goods and enticements bears down on us and threatens to bury us. Continually bombarded by the lure of things, demands for achievement, and philosophies of pleasure, believers may lose their spiritual bearings, become "numb," and start to yield to the overwhelming sensation to give in to the world and resist no more.

But God has called us out of the world; we are "strangers and pilgrims," our brother Peter reminded us (1 Peter 2:11). The warm love and safe haven of Christ's own peace, which the world cannot give us, is the Christian's refuge (John 14:27). The Holy Spirit will lead us to it. The question is, Will we choose to be led?

I. PREPARING TO CLIMB

Evaluate your life in each of the following areas.
- How much time do you spend thinking about—
  how to fulfill your physical needs (e.g., food, pleasure, sex)?

how to get the things you desire (e.g., clothes, car, jewelry, household items)?

how to achieve the recognition you would like to have (e.g., career, awards, position, power)?

• How much money do you spend on—

fulfilling your physical needs?

getting the things you desire?

gaining the honor you'd like to have?

[handwritten: Both Eve & Christ were tempted by Satan in these 3 areas]

II. FINDING A FOOTHOLD

1. To begin our study, read 1 John 2:15-17. What command is given in verse 15? *[handwritten: Stop loving this evil world & all it offers you.]*

[handwritten left margin: lust, materialism, Pride]

2. If we disobey the command, what will be the spiritual result? *[handwritten: you show that we do not love God. We lose sight of loving the Father]*

[handwritten left margin: beautiful, lust of the eye " ", Pride of life, Driver, motivates]

3. Into what three categories does John classify "the world?" *[handwritten: Evil desires, craze for sex, the ambition to buy everything that appeals to you + pride that comes from wealth & importance.]*

4. Why are we told not to love the world? *[handwritten: The world will pass away   The lust of the flesh is evil]*

The "lust of the flesh" is uncontrolled natural appetites (food, drink, sex, pleasure). The "lust of the eye" is a desire for all that is beautiful and desirable. It includes the things and riches this world has to offer. "The pride of life" may be thought of as that which drives, motivates. It substitutes man's power and fame for the heavenly honor God wants to bestow on us.

5. Read Genesis 3:1-6. Explain how Eve was tempted in each of the following areas. (a) The lust of the flesh (v. 6) *[handwritten: Satan tried to show Eve that sin is lovely. The fruit was good for food.]*

[handwritten left margin: Radical Spiritual Amputation]

(b) The lust of the eye (v. 6) *[handwritten: The fruit was pleasant to the eye]*

(c) The pride of life (vv. 5, 6) *[handwritten: Adam & Eve could live as Gods knowing good & evil.]*

As God's children, yet still having "sin in the flesh," we will continually do battle with these three lusts by which Satan and the world lure us away from God. The battle has raged since the Garden of Eden.

6. Read 2 Samuel 11:1-17. (a) What two lusts enticed the king to sin?

Lust of the eye + lust of the flesh
Bathsheba was beautiful.

(b) How did Uriah's behavior contrast with David's?

Uriah practiced self control + discipline
David went to great lengths to hide ↓
didnot

7. Read Isaiah 39:1-8. (a) By which of the three lusts was Hezekiah tempted? *Pride of life*

(b) Why might he have done what he did?

He wanted to impress them + perhaps
to avoid war

8. The Lord wants us to set our hearts on Him, not on earthly treasures. What does God say about worldly possessions in these verses?

Proverbs 11:4 *Riches cannot save our souls, only our love*
+ obedience to God will count

Proverbs 23:5 *worldly wealth is unstable + all your*
riches can be lost

Luke 12:34 *Where your treasure is, there will*
be your heart + thoughts.

9. Read the following verses and explain the perils of worldly attraction.

Our relation
with God
beyond life
is free.

Deuteronomy 8:11-14 (Underline v.18) *+ to forget God + inflate*
our pride. In times of plenty its easy to take
credit our prosperity. Do not forget it is God who blesses us.

Matthew 13:22 *worldly attraction + deceitful riches*
choke out God's Word. The cares of the world
choked out God's Word.

You become very possessive

Luke 12:15-21 *Jesus said that the good life has nothing to do with being wealthy. He neglects the soul & salvation. Where will you spend eternity does.*

1 Timothy 6:9, 10 *It leads to temptation & the love of money. It doesn't bring happiness, Be content with what you have.*

10. Scripture offers many reasons why God wants us to separate ourselves from worldliness. What reasons are presented in these verses?

Matthew 6:24 *A person cannot serve two masters, God & money. The love of money is the first step toward all kinds of sin.*

John 15:19 *The world is our enemy. It hated Jesus & God & it hates the Christian.*

James 4:4 *A believer is an enemy of the world and a friend of God. Pleasures that keep us from pleasing God is sinful, but pleasure in God's rich bounty is good.*

1 Peter 2:9-11 *Our value comes from being one of God's children, not from what we achieve. We have worth because of what God does not because of what we do.*

We are God's chosen people, live like it.

11. A departure from worldly love involves a *choice*. Choose two of the following men and explain how each one *chose* to deny the world and follow God wholeheartedly.

Abram: Genesis 14:14-24 — *Abraham & Lot. Abraham refused to take a reward as he wanted God to be honored & given all the credit for his wealth & whatever he owned or did to be given to God.*

I have to choose God over the world

Daniel: Daniel 5:1-17 *Daniel refused the king's gifts but carried out the work as God's messenger & told what the message meant.*

A little different as Daniel got the reward anyway

Paul: Philippians 3:4-10 *Human achievement, no matter how impressive, cannot earn a person salvation & eternal life with God. It comes only through faith in Christ*

Moses: Hebrews 11:24-26 *Moses refused to be treated as the grandson of the king, but instead chose to share ill-treatment with God's people instead of enjoying the pleasures of sin. He thought it better to suffer for the promised Christ than to own all the treasures of Egypt.*

Moses learned to take a stand.

12. Unfortunately, not everyone chooses to unreservedly follow God. The Old Testament saint Lot, perhaps more than any other Bible person, characterizes the believer whose spiritual life and testimony are neutralized by yielding to the pull of the world. Read Genesis 13:5-13. What choice did Lot make in deciding where to dwell? *Toward the wicked city of Sodom*

13. Read Genesis 14:12 and 19:1. Where was Lot dwelling according to these verses? *In the city of Sodom*

14. Now read Genesis 19:15-25. What are some of the attitudes and actions displayed by Lot that showed his love for the world?

James 1:14 & 15   *Flee every appearance of evil*

15. If you read the rest of Genesis 19, you'll see that Lot's life did not result in spiritual victory and productivity. In fact, Lot's descendants later became the enemies of God's people. According to 2 Peter 2:6-8, what was Lot doing by his lifestyle, though he was unaware of it?

He did have a knowledge of God. He didn't love the Lord enough to follow the Lord.

16. God straightforwardly tells us, "Don't love the world!" (See 1 John 2:15.) Christ wants full possession of us, our total love and devotion. How do these verses give us this command?

Luke 12:29-31

Romans 12:1, 2

2 Timothy 2:4

Titus 2:11-13

17. *How* can we wean our hearts from the love of the world? What instruction is given in Romans 8:4, 5, and 12-14?

18. The spiritual riches that Christ longs to give us cannot be contained by this world! Proverbs 13:7 states, "There is that maketh himself poor, yet hath great riches." What riches do we have as God's children? List as many as you can find from Ephesians 1:3-14.

19. Read 1 Chronicles 29:11-13. How does this passage summarize what we have learned in our Scripture study?

III. PRESSING UPWARD

1. Define "worldliness" in your own words.

2. Brainstorm as a group (or as an individual), listing specifically what the world offers to tempt us in each of the following areas.

(a) The lust of the flesh

(b) The lust of the eye

(c) The pride of life

3. Perhaps someone might ask, "Is it wrong, then, for believers to have and enjoy things? Is it a sin to have money?" Explain what a Christian's attitude toward earthly enticements should be. Read the following verses for help, or use other verses you know to support your answer: Exodus 20:3; 1 Corinthians 6:12, 19, 20; 1 Timothy 6:17, 18.

4. We show what is important to us by how much time we spend thinking about something and how much money we spend on something. With this in mind, what are some of the things you consider most important in your life? How do these things relate to the lust of the flesh, the lust of the eyes, and the pride of life?

5. We are bombarded by things! And let's admit it, for many of us there is a definite pull toward worldly possessions. As children of God, how can we minimize the pull of the world and strengthen our love for the Savior?

*[handwritten: 1. Practice to have an attitude of thankfulness
2. Display thanksgiving
3. Think of spiritual things of the Lord.]*

6. Let's be more specific. In practical terms, what activities should you avoid to minimize worldliness and draw closer to God's desire for you? What attitudes should you cultivate?

[handwritten right margin: Pull away from worldliness & add spiritual thing. Put off & the flatton.]

AVOID THESE ACTIVITIES	CULTIVATE THESE ATTITUDES
Lust of the Flesh	
Lust of the Eyes	
Pride of Life	

[handwritten left margin: Are my goals pulling me closer to God or are they drawing me away from God.]

[handwritten center: Learn to be Godly by practicing it as it doesn't come naturally. Avoiding someone or pleasing people.]

James wrote to believers in his letter not to be a friend of the world; John wrote not to love the world. Remember Lot? He made choices. He cast his eyes toward worldly Sodom and soon became settled and comfortable there. Moses, on the other hand, chose to reject the worldly offerings of Egypt in order to wholeheartedly follow God. What choice will you make?

7. Write a brief prayer to God concerning your attitudes toward the world.

IV. REACHING NEW HEIGHTS

Has God spoken to you through His Word? Spend a few moments in prayer, committing one of the following areas to Him. What *action* can you take to obey Him? Allow Him to work in your life as He enables you to overcome the pull of worldly attractions.

_____ I have been struggling with the lust of the flesh. I need to make a change in the following way: _____ .
I know I will need to yield daily to the Holy Spirit in this area. I'm thanking Christ for His provision of victory.

_____ I need control over the lust of the eyes. I acknowledge my problem in the following area: _____ .
I'm asking God to enable me through His Spirit to make the necessary changes to free me from the world's grip. I want Christ to rule supreme in my heart and be first in my love.

_____ The pride of life is a pull on me in the following way: _____
_____ .

I yield my "honor" to God and recognize that the glory He gives is superior to any earthly glory. Being led by the Spirit, I desire to live for Christ and serve Him in all things.

V. VIEW FROM THE TOP

The world, the flesh, and the Devil together form a "carnal magnet" to pull us away from the Lord. But, praise God, in His wisdom He has provided a way of escape. He has placed His Holy Spirit in each of us, His children, to empower us to live a holy, righteous life. If we are daily led by the Spirit, we will make right choices and have a right perspective about the pleasures and pursuits of this life. May we live so as to express this prayer each day: "Spirit of God, descend upon my heart: / Wean it from earth, through all its pulses move. / Stoop to my weakness, mighty as Thou art, / And make me love Thee as I ought to love" (George Croly).

L E S S O N   1 0

Cast Down That Idol!

"And thou shalt love the Lord thy God with all thy heart, and with all thy soul, and with all thy mind, and with all thy strength: this is the first commandment" (Mark 12:30).

Right on the heels of our last topic, worldliness, follows the matter of idolatry. Idolatry is the intensification and concentration of desire after one particular object. It is creating another "god" that controls us.

The word "idol" usually conjures up an image of a pagan worshiper in some remote land, offering up incense to a stone statue. Certainly this is idolatry, but idol worship abounds in our culture, too, in forms quite different from its pagan counterpart. An idol is anything that we worship, anything that consumes the love and devotion that rightly belongs to our Lord Jesus. It drains the attention that we ought to be giving to Him.

An idol may be a sin, or it may be something good that goes beyond its proper boundaries. The believer refuses to give it up or give it over to God's control. Whatever it is, it looms so large in the heart that it chokes the spiritual life. Oh, we might continue to go through the "motions of devotions" or participate in church activities, but until the idol is cast down, our relationship to Christ will stall. Until we are willing to obey Him about this matter, we will be running on a spiritual treadmill, gaining no new ground.

Casting down the idol is painful, but God wants first place in our hearts. Pause a moment. Pray right now that the Lord will enable you to be obedient as He speaks to your heart about this matter.

I. PREPARING TO CLIMB

Think about your life. Is there a habit that controls you?

Is there any "thing" or activity that you would be unwilling to give up if God wanted you to do so?

Is there any person whom you have not "given over" to God?

Is there a particular talent or ability with which God has blessed you? What is it?

II. FINDING A FOOTHOLD

1. In order to rightly worship and serve God, we must remove any obstacles that keep us from totally, freely loving and obeying Him alone. How do the following verses reflect this truth?

Genesis 35:1-4 *An idol is anything we put before God. Jacob ordered his household to destroy all their idols, as he wanted to solely lean on God for guidance & to have faith in God only.*

Joshua 24:14, 15 *The people had to decide whether to obey the Lord, who had proven His trustworthiness, or obey the local gods, which were man made idols, and their comes a time when we have to take a stand. Will it be God or whatever we love more. Joshua took a stand & told his people "But for me & my house, we will serve the Lord."*

1 Samuel 7:3, 4 *Samuel told the people to determine to serve the Lord, to get rid of their foreign gods & idols. Some forms of idols today are: money, success, material goods, pride or anything that take the place of God in our lives. The Lord alone is worthy of our service & worship, & nothing and we must let nothing rival Him.*

fame
work
pleasure

In your life, an idol is *anything* that has control over your thoughts, attitudes, words, actions, or emotions! That's quite inclusive, but God refuses to share the rule of your life with anyone or anything else. Another term for an idol might be "an emotional addiction," something you can't do without or won't give up.

The law is a blueprint for living, not a method of salvation.

2. What instruction are we given, through God's Word, about such a problem?

Exodus 20:2-5 *You may worship no other god but Me. You should not make yourselves any images of animals, birds or fish. I will not share my affection with any other God.*

Mark 12:30 *We must love God with all of our heart, soul, mind & strength.*

Romans 6:16-18 *We can choose who we want to serve, & pattern ourselves after Him. Without Jesus we would have no choice; but now thanks to Jesus we can choose God as our master.*

Its bad enough to be a servant of sin but do not be a servant of something that is good.

1 Corinthians 6:12 *I can do all things through Christ, who strengthens me, all things are lawful for me. Regardless of what I say, but the one I obey is my master.*

Hebrews 12:1 *Let us run with patience the race that is set before us. The Christian life involves hard work. It requires us to give up whatever endangers our relationship with God. Fix our eyes on Jesus.*

Put away every sin & every weight that so easily besets us.

3. What causes us to "set up idols" and turn our hearts to them? Read Deuteronomy 11:16. What is the cause? What does this mean? *But beware that your hearts do not turn from God to worship other Gods. Our hearts are deceived. We think the idol will meet our need, but only God can provide all we need. Lust of the eyes — Fishing as an example — To lure fish on the line.*

cloud of witnesses are those who have gone before us.

4. Sometimes our idol may be a besetting sin, a wrong that we continually do again and again by choice. We simply give in to temptation each time it presents itself because we take pleasure in the wrong we are doing. We refuse to give it up, although we may even have some desire to do so. How does this affect our relationship with God according to 1 John 1:6-9? *It hinders our fellowship with God. We can't have fellowship with Him if we continue to sin.*

If we are struggling with a besetting sin, we will often hide it from other people. Our conscience tells us it is wrong; the Holy Spirit also convicts us. But we continue in our sin and wouldn't want others, especially Christians, to know of our failure.

Look up & study the "Faith" chpt. in Hebrews

5. What do we learn about "secret sin" in these verses?

Psalm 90:8 *God knows our secret things. We don't need to cover up our sins, He already knows them + willing to listen when we admit our mistakes.*

If you hide your sin you will not prosper

Proverbs 28:13 *To learn from an error, one needs to admit it + confess it to God + He will forgive us for it. We learn from our mistakes.*

Ecclesiastes 12:14 *God will judge us for everything we do, including every hidden thing good or bad. All people will have to stand before God + be judged for what they did in this life. I John 1:9*

Not every idol is a sinful thing. It may be neutral or even a good thing, but we fashion it into an idol. We set it up on the altar of our hearts and begin to love and devote ourselves to it. Isn't it interesting to note that in the Scriptures God does not cast down idols. (The account in 1 Samuel 5:3 and 4 is an exception.) His people must be the ones to do it.

6. Why did the following men cast down idols?

Gideon: Judges 6:24-27 *He did it in obedience to what God told him to do.*

Hezekiah: 2 Kings 18:1-6 *He did it because he trusted very strongly in the Lord + he wanted to follow the Lord in everything + obey all of God's commands*

Josiah: 2 Kings 23:23-25 *He wanted to follow all the laws that were written in the book that Hilkiah the priest found in the temple. Josiah is remembered as Judah's most obedient king. He knowing he was a sinful man, he attacked the causes of sin*

7. In lesson 9 we learned that what we think about reveals what is truly important to us. An idol will begin to dominate and direct our thoughts and sap our time. It dulls, if not deadens, our interest in spiritual things. We delight in it, and it begins to be bigger than God. What do these verses say about our thoughts and affections?

Psalm 40:8 *I delight to do your will for your law is written on my heart. You should desire these things*

Psalm 42:1, 2 *We should delight in doing God's will. Praise Him. Seek Him + restore your life in good fellowship with Him*

Matthew 5 Blessed is the man who hungers + thirst of the righteousness

The same power that raised Christ which is our source of joy. from the dead is the same power I have.

Psalm 104:34 *Have pleasant thoughts of Him;*

Colossians 3:1, 2 *We should set our affections on Christ. Let Christ live within us. Let Heaven fill your thoughts that is to look at life from God's perspective. It causes us to live in harmony with Him.*

8. Perhaps your idol is a person. Have you set all your hopes, expectations, and dreams upon a certain individual? God must come first in your heart, no matter how worthy of your love that person is. Read Genesis 22:1-13. How did Abraham show his total devotion to God? *He obeyed God by being willing to offer his only son Isaac as a sacrifice. The purpose of testing is to strengthen our character & deepen our commitment to God. Through this difficult experience, Abraham learned about his commitment to obey God. He also learned about God's ability to provide.*

9. Anything that the Lord in His goodness gives to us must be given over to Him. If we withhold it from Him in selfishness, for our own control or pleasure, we cannot see God's true blessing on it or us. What was each of the following people willing to give over for God's use?

Moses: Exodus 4:2-5, 20 *Shepherd's rod. It was just an ordinary stick but God used it to teach Moses a lesson. The rod became a serpent. The rod was Moses assurance of God's presence & power*

The widow: 1 Kings 17:1, 10-16 *meal & oil — God has help where we least expect it. He goes beyond our expectations, all we need is faith. This meal & oil was a simple act of faith & it produced a miracle & every miracle begins with an act of faith.* *Faith in action*

The lad: John 6:5-13 *His lunch. never feel that you are too young or old to be of service to God. He takes whatever we can offer Him in time, ability or resources. If we take the first step in making*

It may be that God has given you some talent or ability. This, too, may *ourselves available to Him,* become an idol and must be consecrated to God for His glory, not your *God will* own. Actually, your ability is a small thing to God, Who owns the world. *show us how* The One Who can raise up servants from stones does not need us to do *greatly* His work. But by His grace, He will use us to glorify Himself and accom- *we can* plish His will. *be used to advance the work of His kingdom.*

humbling

10. Read 1 Chronicles 29:1-18. (a) What did David desire to do?

David wanted to build a house of worship.

a (temple)

(b) What question did he ask the people in verse 5? *Who was willing to consecrate his service for the Lord.*

(c) How did they respond (v. 9)? *They offered willingly what they had to give*

(d) What was David's attitude toward the work he was doing (v. 14)? *He was humble, recognizing his & the peoples unworthiness to serve the Lord.*

What have I received that I didn't own? & What from thee? What forgiven this!

(e) What was his attitude toward what had been given to accomplish the work (vv. 12, 14, 16)? *All that was given to do the work came from the Lord & he didn't want the people to forget this.*

11. How will the following verses guide our attitudes toward our talents?

John 3:27 *The ability to do God's work is given from above. God in Heaven appoints each man's work. John had to continue the work God called him to do.*

John 15:5 *any fruit we bear some from Christ & we can do nothing without Him.*

* *Fruit is not limited to soul winning. In this chapter prayer, joy & love are mentioned as fruit. These are qualities of a Christian character.*

Colossians 3:17 *Do all in Christs name, giving thanks. whatever you do or say, let it be as a representative of the Lord Jesus & come with Him into the presence of God the Father to give him your thanks.*

12. What must you do if you are wrestling with a besetting sin? Read James 4:6-10 and list the commands that enable you to be victorious over temptation.

Verse 7 (two commands) *Give yourselves humbly to God. Resist the devil & he will flee from you. Satan is here now and he is trying to win us over to his cause. With the Holy Spirit in our lives, we can resist Satan & he will flee from us.*

Verse 8 (three commands) *Draw near to God Wash your hands (confess) Let your hearts be filled with God. (hate sin)*

How can we draw close to God?
1. *Give yourselves humble to God Realize that you need His forgiveness & be willing to follow His*
2. *Resist the devil - don't allow him to entice & tempt you*
3. *Wash your hands - that is lead a pure life. Replace sin with God purity*
4. *Let there be tears, sorrow & sincere grief for your sins*
5. *Realize your worthlessness - Humble yourselves before God & He will lift you up*

Verse 9 *mourn/ Let there be tears, sorrow + sincere grief. Don't be afraid to express deep sorrow (heartfelt) for them*

Verse 10 *Humble + be lifted up by God*

13. According to James 4:6, what will God give us if we humble ourselves? *more + more strength. God gives strength to the humble. He will lift you up (Grace)*

14. We may need to make a decision to just get rid of certain habits, activities, or things that keep us from being pleasing to God. Read Acts 19:18-20. (a) What action did these Christians take to cleanse their lives? *They confessed their evil deeds.*

(b) What was the result in verse 20? *They took the witchcraft books + charms + burned them, publicly. God Word prevailed.*

15. We who struggle with so many strong desires and "emotional addictions" can find spiritual freedom from the control of earthly idols. Read Romans 13:14 to find the solution and explain how to put this verse into practice. *Ask the Lord Jesus to help you live as you should + Stay away from anything that appears evil — (wild parties, adultery, lust, fighting) Jealousy + lust are listed sins as bad as sins of drunkness + adultery. Make no plans to fulfill.*

16. What kind of allegiance does Christ expect from us? Read Matthew 10:37-39 and summarize these verses in your own words. *Don't neglect your family, but don't neglect your (higher) mission. God should be our first priority. We should be totally committed to God + willing to face anything, even suffering + death for His sake. The more we love this life's rewards (leisure, power, popularity, money) the more we discover how empty they really are. The best way to enjoy life is to let go of all earthly rewards to be free to follow Christ + look forward to His coming so to be forever with Him.*

17. What motivation do we have to put Christ first in our lives, above every person, thing, or desire? What do 1 Peter 1:18 and 19 say? *God paid a ransom to free us from the tyranny of sin. We could not escape from sin on our own, only the life of God's son could free us. Jesus is our ransom.*

III. PRESSING UPWARD

What causes us, even though we are believers, to create idols in our minds and hearts? We read in Deuteronomy 11:16 that we become deceived, thinking something else will satisfy where God seems to fail. In Exodus 32:1 the Israelites "saw that Moses delayed to come down out of the mount" where he was receiving God's commandments. So the people "gathered themselves together unto Aaron, and said unto him, Up, make us gods, which shall go before us; for as for this Moses . . . we wot [know] not what is become of him." If by our own apathy or impatience a vacuum develops in our relationship with God—a lack of total trust in all areas, we may create a god to comfort ourselves. Thus we bring about an emotional addiction, something we look to to get us through the rough spots.

1. What are some of the emotions that we may seek to "mask" by engaging in certain habits and activities? *Fear, loneliness, depression, discouragement, anger, guilt, insecurity.*

2. In James 4:8 we are instructed not to be double minded about our sin but to purify our hearts. God wants us to hate sin as He hates sin. When we continually battle a besetting sin, we give in because of the pleasure we derive from it. What right Scriptural thinking will help purify our double-mindedness about our sin?

Christ died for my sins
Sin has no more right to rule over us
God wants us to be purified of all sin. pure & holy

Romans 6:?
redeem from sins
grasp

3. When tempted, what plan of action must you implement to be an overcomer? *make a choice & refuse to yield to sin.*

Refuse to give in to sin. Look in scripture & find a verse that deals with that may about it & ask the Lord to show you sin. what wrong & how to correct it. Psalms 119:133

Christ used the word of God when he was tempted.

4. Perhaps you have been hiding a sin, especially from other Christians. What must you remember when you do such a thing? *you cannot hide anything from God – not even your secret thoughts. Pray to resist Practise doing good.*

5. What are some of the specific things that may become idols? Here is my list: fantasizing, food, smoking, drinking, using drugs, shopping, busyness, watching television or a particular television program, a radio program, a computer, reading suggestive or explicit literature, lottery, bingo, rock music, a sport or sports team, a hobby, a certain form of entertainment or relaxation, accumulating things, a job or career, impure activities, a goal, a relationship with a person. Add anything else that comes to your mind. *Reading the newspaper in the morning before I have my devotions.*

6. After a woman has identified an idol in her life, she must let God's Word and His Spirit transform her thinking, attitudes, and actions. How can she do this? (Refer to Section II, questions 5 and 6, for help.) *Idolatry is sin & sin must be dealt with. Repent. Use self control. Put off the idol, put on spiritual thoughts.*

7. When giving over an idol to God, a common emotion is fear. ("How can I do without this?" Such a feeling shows a dependence of

sorts and indicates we are putting our trust in the idol rather than God.) This is especially true if the idol is a person. What fears do we usually have about "giving over" someone we love to God?

Matthew 10: 37 says, If you love father or mother, more than you love me, you are not worthy of me

8. How will casting down idols bring us freedom in spirit? Read John 4:24. *If we worship anything else we are not free to worship God.*

9. What talent or ability do you have? How can it be given over to God for His glory in your life?

10. Perhaps you suspect there is an idol in your heart. May I suggest a test? Suppose God were to tell you, "I want you to give this up." How would you react? Would you say, "I can't!" or "I don't want to"? Or could you open your hand and heart and reply, "Yes, Father. Here it is if You want it. I give it up for You"? Did this test enable you to detect an idol in your heart?

11. What will keep us from idols? "Saturation" with Christ is the answer. Love Him first, love Him most. Fill your heart with Him. Surprisingly, we can love Him with the whole heart and still have love (His love in us) for all that is proper. How can you increase your love for Christ today?

1. By Prayer
Loving Him more
2. By Serving.
3. By spending time in the Word & applying it.

IV. REACHING NEW HEIGHTS

Has God spoken to you through His Word? Spend a few moments in prayer, committing one of the following areas to Him. What *action* can you take to obey Him? Allow Him to work in your life as He enables you to overcome the sin of idolatry.

_____ The Lord has convicted me that I have made an idol out of

_____ .

> By God's grace, I now give this idol over to Him. I desire Christ to have first place in my life and the freedom that comes from not being controlled by any other person or thing.

_____ The Lord has blessed me with this ability: _____

_____ .

> I am giving it over to His control and desiring to use it for His glory. I will continue to pray that I will display the humility of Christ in this matter.

V. VIEW FROM THE TOP

I have had to deal with idolatry in my own life, and perhaps God has been putting His finger on something in your life that is causing you to step out of His will. It may well be that God has been convicting you about this idol for some time but that you have refused to obey. Or it may be that the light of God's Word has just made you aware of your idolatry.

Don't be afraid to give this idol over to God. Don't convince yourself that "it's just a little thing; it won't hurt." Jesus Christ, Who bought you with His own blood, wants to be first in your love (Revelation 2:4). When He controls us, nothing else can. "Little children, keep yourselves from idols. Amen" (1 John 5:21).

In the Snare of Self-deceit

"Let us search and try our ways, and turn again to the
LORD" (Lamentations 3:40).

The world, the flesh, and the Devil are the believer's constant
adversaries, sources of continual pressure to live an ungodly life. *Spiritual Problems*
But "his divine power hath given unto us all things that pertain unto life
and godliness" (2 Peter 1:3). Thankfully, that power is at work in us
through the Holy Spirit, Who enables us to overcome sin as we yield to
Him.

But what if we don't yield and we do sin? And what if we find
ourselves sinning repeatedly? We must, of course, come back to God and
be cleansed. Only then can we live freely and honestly before Him.

Nevertheless, we may stop confessing, and sin may begin to run
rampant in our lives. We stop yielding and stop caring; we begin to deal
with our guilt and conviction by covering up. Since "man looketh on the
outward appearance" (1 Samuel 16:7), we are concerned that we look
good on the outside. We begin to playact what a Christian should be.
(This, by the way, is what the word "hypocrite" means.) Meanwhile, on
the inside, we deny our true condition by shifting the blame, making
excuses, justifying, or judging others for their failures. Alas! We are
caught in the snare of self-deceit! Being far from the truth, which makes
us free, we are in a wretched trap that holds us securely.

How can we find release? God, our Father Who knows us so well, has
placed the key into our very own hands! Are we willing to use it?

Life dominating sins are evil desires

I. PREPARING TO CLIMB

Are you a person who

—has a difficult time saying "I'm sorry"?

—seldom asks forgiveness?

—sees others as the cause of your reactions?

—makes excuses for the wrong you do?

—judges others harshly for their failures?

—becomes defensive if corrected?

—avoids telling your spiritual struggles to another?

II. FINDING A FOOTHOLD

There is joy when you know you don't need to carry a burden

One of the joys of being a Christian is honestly looking at ourselves, acknowledging the sin we see, confessing it, and knowing we are cleansed. Then we can proceed through life with the burden of sin removed and left behind. What freedom! Unfortunately, the sin in us often fights against repentance. Even as Christians we hide our sin from ourselves and others. The source of this action, of course, is pride.

Read James 1:21–27 and answer the following questions.

1. What is the proper response to God's Word (vv. 21, 22, 25)?

Do what it says

2. How does a believer deceive herself (vv. 22, 23, 26)?

3. What will show genuine obedience to God's Word (vv. 21-27)?

Obeying & getting rid of the sin in my life.

4. Read Jeremiah 17:9. Why do we deceive ourselves about our sin? (See also Romans 7:18-20.)

5. Read 1 John 1:9 and 2:6 carefully. This passage is written to believers. (Note that John wrote "we" and "my little children.") In our relationship with God, as our Father, what does He always want His children to do with sin? *When I have wrong thoughts, I need to confess it & repent.*

6. According to 1 John 1:10, what is true of us if we deny that we commit sin? *We are calling God a liar.*

7. In 1 John 2:1 and 2 what provision has God made for the cleansing of every sin? *The sacrifice of Jesus Christ, His Son.*

8. What "fruit" does the Father expect to see in the lives of His obedient children, as stated in 1 John 2:3-6? *Obedience to His Word.*

9. Telltale attitudes reveal a person who is refusing to acknowledge sin in her life. What attitudes are described in these verses?

Proverbs 12:15 *will not take the Word of God to see their own sin.*

Matthew 7:3, 4 *sees other sin but not their own*

James 3:14-16 *Bitter envy & their desire is to be better than anyone else.*

10. Scripture always gives us vivid, real-life examples of sin, as well as of holiness. Read each passage and describe how the person reacted when confronted with his or her sin.

- Genesis 3:1-13 *Adam blamed Eve. Eve blamed the serpent*

  Adam (v. 12) *Am I my brother's keeper?*

  God gave him an opportunity to confess but he didn't want to.

  Eve (v. 13)

- Genesis 4:3-9

  Cain (v. 9)

- Exodus 32:1-6, 21-24

  Aaron (vv. 22, 24) *Golden calf*

- 1 Samuel 13:5-13 *I felt compelled to offer a burnt offering.*

  Saul (vv. 11, 12)

Apply God's Word to little things, so when the big thing comes about God lets us handle it.

11. When we refuse to acknowledge our sin before God, when we harden our hearts to the Spirit's conviction, we will suffer consequences. We always reap what we sow (Galatians 6:7). What are some of the consequences of a Christian's sinful living?

Proverbs 28:13 *If we conceal our sins we will not prosper*

Proverbs 28:14 *He who hardens his heart will fall into trouble.*

John 15:4-6 *If I do not confess my sin I will not have joy etc—*

1 John 2:28 *I will be ashamed at Christ's return.*

12. (a) In a graphic Old Testament passage, God describes Israel's attitudes and reactions when He confronted her about her sins. Read Zechariah 7:8-13. How did the Lord "speak" to Israel (v. 12)?

(b) What were some of the changes God wanted Israel to make (vv. 9, 10)?

(c) How did Israel react to God's rebuke (vv. 11, 12)?

(d) What attitudes would you say Israel manifested?

13. Attitudes! They determine whether we will spiritually stall or take off! Look up the following verses and explain what kind of response God wants you to have when confronted about your sin. *Israel did not respond right.*

Proverbs 14:29
Think about, don't get angry.
Proverbs 9 - Rebuke

Lamentations 3:39-42
Don't complain, examining your heart.

1 Corinthians 11:28-31

Examine + judge your own life, so God doesn't have to judge you. God always forgives sin, but not the consequences of that sin.

Proverbs - 7

Psalm 51:17

2 Corinthians 7:9, 10

Godly sorrow is one of brokenness

When a Christian woman refuses to face the sin in her life and pretends to be spiritually sound, the result is inner wretchedness. The sinning Christian may work hard to keep up appearances before others, lest anyone realize that her "secret" life is not what it should be. The result is often emotional exhaustion, physical distress, and spiritual bondage. But as the Savior reminded us, whatever is in the heart will eventually show itself in words and actions (Matthew 12:34, 35). How much better to be free! David knew this after he tried to hide his sins relating to Bathsheba (adultery, lying, murder).

14. Read Psalm 32. (a) How did David feel when he denied his sin (vv. 3, 4)? *His bones crumbled*

Psalms 51:11-13

(b) How did he feel upon confessing his sin? *I have sinned against God. He was joyful*

15. In section II you read James 3:14-16. Reread that passage, adding verses 13, 17, and 18. In general, if you are living a clean and confessed life, what kind of person should you be right now?

III. PRESSING UPWARD

1. Although a Christian is unlikely to deny being a sinner, she may re-

sist acknowledging *specific* sins. List as many reasons as you can why people deny their sins to themselves or others.

2. We read in Zechariah 7 that God spoke to Israel about her sin by means of the Law, His Spirit, and the prophets. When we continue in sin, how will God speak to us about it?

3. Israel turned her back and stopped up her ears. Obviously, we wouldn't sit in church with our fingers in our ears as the pastor preaches! Our defiance is much more creative and subtle than that. In what ways will a believer avoid being convicted by God's Word?

4. As we saw in our study of Old Testament people, exposure to sin brings varied reactions. Explain as best you can *why* people might react in each of these ways.

(a) Become defensive

(b) Shift the blame

(c) Make excuses

(d) Spiritualize

(e) Judge others harshly

5. Have you figured out yet what is the key to release from the snare of self-deceit? It is repentance. Second Corinthians 7:9 and 10 speak of "worldly sorrow" and "godly sorrow" (which leads to repentance). What is the difference?

6. Why is an unrepentant believer so wretched? Do you think she truly realizes it?

7. When a sinning Christian repents and turns back to God, what attitudes, words, and actions would you expect to see? (For insight, read 2 Samuel 12:1-24 and Psalm 51:3-9.)

8. James 5:16 says, "Confess your faults one to another, and pray one for another, that ye may be healed." The word "faults" means "missing the mark, failure." What are the spiritual benefits of confessing our faults to another confidential, godly believer?

When was the last time you confessed a fault (spiritual failure) to another believer? If you are trying to present a righteous facade— "everything's okay with me"—a warning signal should sound in your heart. Because the heart is deceitful, we all have areas in which we fail to see our sin. The first question you should *honestly* ask yourself is, Do I really want to be free from my sinful thoughts, attitudes, words, and actions? If not, you must begin by asking God to change your will and give you a desire for holiness. But if you do want to repent of sin, what must you do to bring that about in your life?

9. Write a prayer that expresses to God what He has shown you through His Word in this lesson.

IV. REACHING NEW HEIGHTS

Has God spoken to you through His Word? Spend a few moments in prayer, committing one of the following areas to Him. What *action* can you take to obey Him? Allow Him to work in your life as He enables you to escape the snare of self-deceit.

_____ The Lord has made me aware that I have been denying the sin in my life. I have been making excuses and justifying many sinful attitudes, words, and actions. I am asking the Lord to cleanse me, and I am turning to Him with a new desire to obey Him and grow in His holiness.

_____ The Lord has convicted me about some areas of sin with which I have been refusing to deal. I am confessing these to Him right now and am seeking to yield to His power to live righteously in these areas.

_____ I am praying that the Lord will show me any areas of sin about which I have been deceiving myself. I want to live in the freedom of a clean life, and I know that God will be faithful to keep me growing as I live openly and honestly before Him.

V. VIEW FROM THE TOP

You walk into church, looking prim and acting pleasant. You sing the hymns, give your tithe, read the Scripture, look attentively at the pastor when he preaches. You hear the Word, *God's* Word, but you do not allow it to penetrate your inmost being. To have to acknowledge your guilt, the sin that is there, would be painful, humiliating. So you shove the conviction aside, and church is "done" for another week. You go back to your home, criticize your husband, vent your anger at the children, gossip at work. No one at church knows what you're really like. In fact, your sin seems so normal that you've deceived yourself. After all, you go to church; you must be a pretty good Christian.

But Christ looks into the heart; there is no deceiving Him. He wants to free you from this futile pattern of life, but escape begins only when you are willing to humble yourself, tell Him honestly about all your sin, and seek His grace to be changed. He will do the changing if you hold out empty hands, desiring His will.

If this describes your life at present, don't delay another day. Pride and fear will keep you from admitting your spiritual need. But don't you long for the joy and peace that an open, cleansed life can bring? Escape the snare! Be free! Wear the mask no longer! Become the godly woman Christ intends you to be.

Choose ye this day whom you will serve.

The Joy of Overcoming

If you do not get food from communing with God, you can't expect the church to do the growing for you.

Think right Do right & you will feel right

Put off & then Put on

"Wherefore seeing we also are compassed about with so great a cloud of witnesses, let us lay aside every weight, and the sin which doth so easily beset us, and let us run with patience the race that is set before us, Looking unto Jesus the author and finisher of our faith; who for the joy that was set before him endured the cross, despising the shame, and is set down at the right hand of the throne of God" (Hebrews 12:1, 2).

The Rocky Mountains, the Sierra Nevadas—both are mountain ranges of indescribable beauty. But to early American pioneers, they were also treacherous. With these great obstacles looming across the horizon, what hope was there to safely reach the land of new opportunity and plenty? Providentially, a group of about six hundred men, known as "the Mountain Men," used their skill and strength to overcome the menace of the mountains. They marked out the best routes, explored the rivers, and discovered the necessary passes through the mountains. Some of the men even acted as guides to the wagon trains. Where success had seemed impossible, the Mountain Men opened a way.

When success in the Christian life seems impossible, we must realize that Jesus Christ has totally provided the way. As God, He has used His divine power to throw down every obstacle from earth to Heaven. As man, He understands the trials we face because He has trod the same path before us. "For in that he himself hath suffered being tempted, he is able to succour them that are tempted" (Hebrews 2:18).

106

Yes, Christ is *the* overcomer, and He can and will enable us to overcome all spiritual obstacles. When we keep our eyes on Him and determine to follow, He will lead us all the way. And what joy there is in each victorious step! *Christ will give us the victory.*

I. PREPARING TO CLIMB

On a scale of 1 to 10 (10 being the best), rate yourself, at present, on the following qualities as described in the following statements.

__8__ FREEDOM from sin. I specifically confess my sins to God daily, and I am desiring to live a holy life in thoughts, attitudes, words, and actions.

__7__ FAITH. I am trusting in the greatness of God to enable me to overcome my inner and outward obstacles.

__8__ FOCUS. My thoughts are often filled with Christ and His Word.

__7__ FERVENCY. I am daily seeking to know God more fully, love Him more deeply, and obey Him more completely.

__6__ FAITHFULNESS. I am carrying out the responsibilities God has given me in all areas of life and am doing them for His glory.

II. FINDING A FOOTHOLD

FREEDOM from sin! This should be a growing reality in the life of every Christian. Jesus said, "Ye shall know the truth, and the truth shall make you free" (John 8:32). The truth of the gospel (1 Corinthians 15:1-4), when received, sets us free from God's wrath and an eternity in Hell. Have you received God's gift of eternal life and forgiveness of sin? If not, you are really not free, but a slave of Satan. Receive Christ into your life today, and He will set you free to love and follow Him.

The truth of God's Word, when applied to our lives as believers, sets us free from sin in the flesh that seeks to control us. By position, we have already been set free from sin's right to rule over us (Romans 6), but by our own choice, we obey sin once more.

1. What assurance is given in the following verses that God wants us
to experience victory over sin?

1 Corinthians 10:13 *God is faithful & will not allow us to be tempted above what we are able to bear. He will also find a way to escape.*

2 Corinthians 2:14 *God always causes us to triumph (Victory) in Christ.*

James 4:7 *If we put ourselves under Gods' authority, & resist Satan, he will flee from us. With the Holy Spirit's power lives we can resist Satan and he will flee from us.*

Stand firm!

2. According to Hebrews 4:15 and 16, how is Christ Jesus both our
model and deliverer with regard to victory over sin? *He was tempted in every area that we are; yet He didn't sin, If we came to Him for help against temptation, He will give us grace & mercy to help.*

3. There is joy when we have freedom from sin! But what enables a
believer to overcome sin? Look up these verses and record your findings.

Psalm 119:11 *God's Word being in our hearts & minds. Storing God's Word in our hearts & minds is a deterrent to sin. This alone should inspiring us to want to memorize scripture; this will help to put God's Word to work in our lives.*

Hide His Word in your heart

Matthew 26:41 *Being Alert to temptation & praying that we will not give in. Keep alert & pray, otherwise temptation will empower you. For the spirit is willing, but how weak the body is.*

Watch & Pray. Be alert to sin.

Romans 6:12-14 *Having a yielded life. We recognize we are no longer under sin's authority, but God's. We now have grace to overcome sin.*

Galatians 5:16 *Moment by moment we must walk in the Spirit. Obey the Spirits directions, He will tell you where to go & what to do & then you won't always be doing the wrong things your evil nature wants you to.*

Most of the topics presented in this study have dealt with negative
aspects of our lives: pride, fear, bitterness, idolatry. While it is important
to face the presence of these sins, overcoming spiritual obstacles requires
many positive acts of the will. The first of these is FAITH. With faith we
don't just climb mountains, we move them (Matthew 17:20)! Biblical
faith always centers on the being and character of God.

4. According to the following verses, how will faith enable you to
overcome spiritual obstacles?

Ephesians 6:16 *Faith is a shield to ward off attacks of Satan. By faith I can resist Satan*

James 1:2-4 *When our faith is tested & strengthened we develop spiritual endurance, which leads to maturity in Christ. God promises to be with us at all times.*

1 John 5:4, 5 — *By our faith in Christ, we have already overcome the world. I've already won the victory.*

5. Read Luke 4:1-13. How does a life of faith, as reflected by our Savior, enable us to deal with temptation? *He was filled with the Holy Spirit's power (we can be too). He knew God's word & how to use it against Satan temptations. He could not be swayed from putting His whole trust in His father. By faith, He defeated Satan. (We can too.)*

6. What qualities will fill our hearts when we have faith? Read Romans 15:13. *Hope, joy & peace in believing. Joy & Peace if I am walking in faith*

A dear saint of the past, John Fletcher, once said, "The work of sanctification is hindered . . . by holding out the being delivered from sin as the mark to be aimed at, instead of being rooted in Christ and filled with the power [of God] from on high." I am learning that when Christ is my FOCUS, when my heart and mind are saturated with Him, then I *will* sin less. This, then, is really the solution to the obstacles presented in this study: give yourself fully to know, love, and obey Christ.

7. Select one of the following passages and explain how it urges you to focus on the Lord Jesus.

1 Corinthians 1:30, 31 *Christ is your source of wisdom, righteousness & wisdom. I am nothing without Jesus Christ.*

Philippians 3:7-10 *Knowing Christ, surpasses all earthly gain, everything else is nothing in comparison to knowing Him & being like Him.*

Colossians 3:16, 17 *All your service is to be done for Him. The Word of God should take over your whole life.*

1 Peter 2:21-25 *Christ is our example in suffering, in holiness, in submission & in sacrifice. He is our source of righteousness & comfort.*

8. Christ is our focus; we are urged in Scripture to "consider him" (Hebrews 12:3). Read Hebrews 2:18; 3:1, 2; and 12:1-3. (a) What qualities of Christ should we think upon when we feel we cannot overcome? *A. He is merciful & faithful, He has suffered & He can help us.*
B. Come boldly to the Throne of Grace for help

(b) What should we do at such times, as directed in Hebrews 4:15 and 16?

Perhaps the greatest challenge we face as Christians is to maintain our spiritual FERVENCY. It seems we must continually strive to keep our "hearts hot" and our "faith on fire." The slide toward spiritual complacency is easy when we become tired, busy, or overwhelmed.

9. What is Christ's desire as He implied it in Revelation 2:4? *He wants to be our first love.*

10. When Christ is our focus, we will be fervent. In what ways will we be fervent according to the following verses?

Matthew 22:37 *Fervently love God.*

Hebrews 11:6 *Fervently seek Him*

Psalm 119:140, 162, 167 *Fervently love His Word.*

1 Thessalonians 5:17; Ephesians 6:18 *Fervently pray*

Luke 6:35; Hebrews 13:16 *Fervently do good*

Psalm 100:2; Colossians 3:23 *Fervently serve*

2 Corinthians 7:1; 1 Peter 1:15 *Fervently seek holiness,*

1 Peter 3:15 *Fervently witness.*

11. (a) How was our Lord a model of fervent obedience as He lived on earth? Summarize His attitude as expressed in John 4:34 and 9:4. *His desire to accomplish God's will with each moment of His life. He longed to do His Father's will*

(b) What was His response when God's will was accomplished? See Luke 10:21. *Joy in His spirit.*

As we live by faith, maintaining our focus and our fervency, we will experience the joy of FAITHFULNESS. What blessedness to realize what God has done in us and through us as we've walked with Him over weeks, months, and years!

12. In what ways will faithfulness reveal itself? Write down your answers from these verses.

Be ready & prepared

2 Timothy 2:19-21 *We will depart (Turn) from sin iniquity. We will be suitable for the Master's use & ready to work for Him. Ready for God to use us.*

Hebrews 10:23-25 *We will be stedfast in the faith. We will encourage other believers. We will be regular in church attendance. Faithful*

James 5:7, 8 *We will patiently wait for God to work out His purposes. We will be mindful of Christ' return.*

13. Hebrews 2:17 and 3:2 remind us of the faithfulness of our Great High Priest. According to Hebrews 12:2, what was one motivation for Christ's being faithful? *The joy of finishing well.*

14. What encouragement do these verses give us in our desire to be faithful?

1 Corinthians 15:57, 58 *God always gives us the Victory, so we should be stedfast & work for Him.*

Philippians 1:6 *As we try to be faithful to Him, He is faithfully working in us.*

1 Thessalonians 5:23, 24 *God is faithful to sanctify us & keep us until redemption.*

15. Read Romans 8:35-37. How do these verses cause you to realize that you *are* an overcomer in Christ? *Nothing can separate us from the love christ has for us & through Him we are more than conquerors.*

III. PRESSING UPWARD

1. How does freedom from sin bring joy to our lives? *Through a clear concience, decrease of conflicts & problems, knowing we are pleasing God.* *Prov. 28:1*

2. God's Word is central in the battle of the Christian life. To neglect it is to be as vulnerable as a soldier going into a battle without his *Prov. 13:15*

Sin brings hard times *# Tim. 5:9*

weapon. Sadly, we often do neglect His Word. Why? List as many reasons as you can. *Busyness, too many detractions (kids, phone, too difficult to understand. Don't know where to begin. (What are the solutions to these problems?)*

3. Brainstorm: How many ways can you learn about the Bible? List them. *Read, study, memorize scripture, go to S.S. Go to church, Bible study, listen to worship station.*

Select one of the ways that would help you grow deeper in your knowledge of Scripture. What sacrifice would you have to make to do this?

4. Our faith deepens as we grow in our understanding of Who God is and what He is willing and able to do in our lives. What are some *practical*, everyday things that you can do to strengthen your faith in the Lord? *Ask God to increase your faith, Read the Word. Read biographies of great men. Keep a record of answered prayer. Read the Psalms & Proverbs. Memorize scripture. Read good books. Biographies. Share your blessings.*

5. Our daily aim should be to focus on Christ; the hindrance is often our busyness! In Psalm 46:10 the Lord tells us, "Be still, and know that I am God." How can we create moments of worship in the course of our busy lives? *Set a specific time to Bible reading + prayer also memorize scripture verses.*

For many Christians, fervency equals service (remember Martha?). They think that the busier they are in church, the more fervent is their love for the Lord. But Christians can be very active and not be loving Christ as they should, nor being Spirit-led in their hearts. (Read Revelation 2:2-5.) Actually, some Christians are so burned out from working that they are spiritually out of gas. They are running on empty. (Telltale sign: no JOY!)

6. What can we, as Christian women, do to minimize this kind of burnout? How are we to maintain true spiritual fervency? *Step back & evaluate our lives. Learn to say (No)*

7. Faithfulness to Christ brings joy! Think of a believer you know who is joyful. How has he or she been faithful to Christ?

8. In what ways has Christ enabled you to overcome spiritual obstacles in the past? *By examples in Scripture Promises in His Word Prayer Support of other believers.*

9. Think back over the lessons in this study: pride, discouragement, fear, bitterness, ingratitude, worldliness, idolatry, self-deceit. About which obstacle were you most greatly convicted by the Spirit? Are you making progress in overcoming? By what means are you obtaining the victory? (Remember, the battle may be ongoing, but Christ is a faithful High Priest!)

IV. REACHING NEW HEIGHTS

Has God spoken to you through His Word? Spend a few moments in prayer, committing one of the following areas to Him. What *action* can you take to obey Him? Allow Him to fill your heart with joy as He enables you to be an overcomer!

_____ Lord, as I end this study, I realize I have never truly received Christ as my Savior and Lord. I am going to put my faith in Him right now, trusting in His death and resurrection as the payment for my sins and receiving God's gift of eternal life. I am asking You to come into my life.

_____ Lord, I have become aware through Your Word that I have some deep struggles with sin. I want to be free from these burdens. Enable me to overcome as I surrender my life to Your control, study Your Word, and pray.

_____ Lord, increase my faith. I want to have a deeper trust in Your faithfulness and power.

_____ Lord, teach me how to be focused on You all the day long. Let my mind be filled with Christ and be rooted in Him so that I may respond as He would in every situation.

_____ Lord, I want to be fervent. I have been struggling with inconsistency and complacency. When I am tired, remind me to rest and take more time to read the Bible and pray. At low times, I will pray for Your Spirit to rekindle the flame in my heart.

_____ Lord, I want to be faithful. Help me to understand the responsibilities that *You* want me to do—and then to do them for *Your* glory.

V. VIEW FROM THE TOP

We could be selfish in our thinking about all that Christ does for us. We do have freedom, joy, peace, and hope as He delivers us from sin and this present evil world. But our lives as overcomers are meant to be an attraction to unbelievers, to cause them to wonder about the "hope that is in you" (1 Peter 3:15). As Paul declared in 2 Corinthians 2:14, "Now thanks be unto God, which always causeth us to triumph in Christ, and maketh manifest the savour of his knowledge by us in every place." Yes, by our lives—our freedom, faith, focus, fervency, and faithfulness, as well as our joy—we ought to be pointing the world to our Savior and Lord, Jesus Christ.

> Keep me,
> > O Lord,
> from being a camouflage Christian,
> from blendingmeltingmerging with
> the muddled mess
> of humanity's self-centeredness.
> Make
> > me
> > > pure vibrancy.
> Give me,
> > I pray,
> a vivid, shocking faith
> that strikes the sightless eyes
> of the world and
> jolts
> them to see
> > > THEE.

Conclusion

I will never forget that bright, brisk, snowy day and the experience I had of climbing a mountain! In my college days I was attending a retreat in the Pocono Mountains of Pennsylvania. Two enthusiastic girls invited me to join them in a hike up to one of the nearby ridges. It was not too perilous, but the day was cold and the trek strenuous (especially for one not in condition for such activity!).

But the labor was well worth the effort. Upon conquest, we sat on the ridge, gazing in wonder at the scene before us: row after row of muted winter-cloaked mountains, a deep snow-covered vale before us, a small herd of deer running silently through a distant wood. What quiet joy filled our hearts in that moment!

The spiritual life of a Christian is like traveling over a mountain range. Life is not all valleys, nor is it all mountaintop experiences. It is a series of ups and downs, a pattern of struggles and—hopefully—victories.

In our quest to reach the top of the next mountain, a new spiritual triumph, we must overcome the immediate spiritual obstacles in our lives. God is faithful to show us what they are if we are open and attentive to His voice. The Lord Jesus is with us in our climb. The Holy Spirit gives us power to make it, and the Bible will give us direction. Victory over every obstacle is assured if we trust and obey.

When we reach the top—what exhilaration! In quiet wonder we worship God for what He is able to do in us. His promises are sure; the obstacles *can* be overcome. The spiritual labor is well worth the effort.

What mountain are you climbing right now? Are you nearing the top, or are you meandering through a tangled valley below? In Christ, you *are* an overcomer. "It is God that girdeth me with strength, and maketh my way perfect. He maketh my feet like hinds' feet, and setteth me upon my high places" (Psalm 18:32, 33). Dear sister in Christ, keep on climbing!

LEADER'S GUIDE

SUGGESTIONS FOR LEADERS

The Bible is a living and powerful book! It is God speaking to us today. Every opportunity to learn from it is a precious privilege. As you use this study guide, be flexible. It is simply a tool to aid in the understanding of God's Word. Adapt it to suit your unique group of women and their needs. The discussion questions are optional; the answers are provided to clarify my intent and stimulate your thought. You may have an entirely different insight as the Holy Spirit illumines your heart and mind.

Each section of the study has a specific purpose.

The *introductory paragraphs* furnish background information and lead in to the topic of that lesson.

The answers to the questions in *Section I* (Preparing to Climb) are personal and should not be discussed in the group. They will help prepare each woman's heart to receive God's Word as she does her own study.

Section II (Finding a Foothold) is aimed at studying the actual text of Scripture and understanding what it says.

The answers to the questions in *Section III* (Pressing Upward) should help to focus on various applications of the passage for that lesson.

Section IV (Reaching New Heights) is not for group discussion. The suggested decisions are starting points for each lady to put God's truth into practice in her own life. You should close the session in prayer, asking God to bring lasting fruit from your study of His Word.

Section V (View from the Top) will help to seal in your mind what you have learned from the passage.

The effectiveness of a group Bible study usually depends on two things: (1) the leader herself and (2) the ladies' commitment to prepare beforehand and interact during the study. You cannot totally control the second factor, but you have total control over the first one. These brief suggestions will help you be an effective Bible study leader.

You will want to prepare each lesson a week in advance. During the week, read supplemental material and look for illustrations in the everyday events of your life as well as in the lives of others.

Encourage the ladies in the Bible study to complete each lesson before the meeting itself. This preparation will make the discussion more interesting.

Also encourage the ladies to memorize the key verse or verses for each lesson. (The verse is printed below the title of each lesson.) If possible, print the verses on 3" x 5" cards to distribute each week. If you cannot do this, suggest that the ladies make their own cards and keep them in a prominent place throughout the week.

The physical setting in which you meet will have some bearing on the study itself. An informal circle of chairs, chairs around a table, someone's living room or family room— these types of settings encourage people to relax and participate. In addition to an informal setting, create an atmosphere in which ladies feel free to participate and be themselves.

During the discussion time, here are a few things to observe.

• Don't do all the talking. This is not designed to be a lecture.

• Encourage discussion on each question by adding ideas and questions.

• Don't discuss controversial issues that will divide the group. (Differences of opinion are healthy; divisions are not.)

• Don't allow one lady to dominate the discussion. Use statements such as these to draw others into the study: "Let's hear from someone on this side of the room" (the side opposite the dominant talker); "Let's hear from someone who has not shared yet today."

• Stay on the subject. The tendency toward tangents is always possible in a discussion. One of your responsibilities as the leader is to keep the group on the track.

• Don't get bogged down on a question that interests only one person.

You may want to use the last fifteen minutes of the scheduled time for prayer. If you have a large group of ladies, divide into smaller groups for prayer. You could call this the "Share and Care Time."

If you have a morning Bible study, encourage the ladies to go out for lunch with someone else from time to time. This is a good way to get acquainted with new ladies. Occasionally you could plan a time when ladies bring their own lunches or salads to share and eat together. These things help promote fellowship and friendship in the group.

The formats that follow are suggestions only. You can plan your own format, use one of these, or adapt one of these to your needs.

2-hour Bible Study

10:00—10:15 Coffee and fellowship time
10:15—10:30 Get-acquainted time
             Have two ladies take five minutes each to tell something about themselves and their families.
             Also use this time to make announcements and, if appropriate, take an offering for the babysitters.
10:30—11:45 Bible study
             Leader guides discussion of the questions in the day's lesson.
11:45—12:00 Prayer time

2-hour Bible Study

10:00—10:45 Bible lesson
             Leader teaches a lesson on the content of the material. No discussion during this time.
10:45—11:00 Coffee and fellowship
11:00—11:45 Discussion time
             Divide into small groups with an appointed leader for each group. Discuss the questions in the day's lesson.
11:45—12:00 Prayer time

1¹/₂-hour Bible Study
10:00—10:30 Bible study
         Leader guides discussion of half the questions in the day's lesson.
10:30—10:45 Coffee and fellowship
10:45—11:15 Bible study
         Leader continues discussion of the questions in the day's lesson.
11:15—11:30 Prayer time

ANSWERS FOR LEADER'S USE

Information inside parentheses ( ) is additional instruction for the group leader.

LESSON 1

Section II—1. *Romans 3:23*—We have all sinned; we have come short of glorifying God. *Ephesians 4:18*—Our understanding of God is darkened; we are alienated from God, are ignorant of spiritual things, have blindness of heart. *John 8:34*—We are servants of sin. *Ephesians 2:1*—We are dead in trespasses and sins. *Isaiah 59:2*—We are separated from God by our sin.

2. *Romans 6:23*—Death. (Leader: Explain that "death" in the spiritual sense means eternal separation from God. All people, Christians included, die a physical death due to Adam's sin, the Fall.) *2 Thessalonians 1:7-9*—The vengeance of God will be upon her; punished with everlasting destruction from the presence of the Lord. (*Discuss:* Why do the holiness and righteousness of God make it necessary that sin be punished?)

3. *Romans 3:10-12*—There is no one who is righteous and seeks after God (apart from His working in a person); there is no one who does good. *Titus 3:5*—Works of righteousness do not save us from God's judgment; we are dependent on His mercy. (Leader: Define "mercy." It is God's goodness and love toward the guilty that allows Him to not give us what we do deserve.) *Matthew 7:21-23*—Many people expect to enter Heaven based on good deeds done in Jesus' name, but since they do not know Him (i.e., have a personal faith relationship with Him) their good deeds are considered iniquity. *Isaiah 64:6*—All of our own "righteousnesses" (efforts to make ourselves look righteous) is filthy in God's eyes. *2 Timothy 1:8, 9*—God does not save us based on our works, but by His purpose and grace.

4. *John 3:17*—God sent Jesus not because He wanted to condemn the people of the world, but because He wanted to save them. *1 Corinthians 15:3*—Christ died for our sins according to the Scriptures. *1 Peter 3:18*—Christ died for our sins to bring us to God. *Romans 5:8*—God showed how much He loved us by Christ's dying for us.

5. *Romans 1:4*—It proved He is the Son of God in power. *1 Corinthians 15:3-6*—Christ's death, burial, and resurrection fulfilled the Old Testament Scriptures of the Messiah. *1 Peter 1:3*—It gives us hope that we will be resurrected too.

6. *John 1:12*—Receive, believe. *John 6:47*—Believe. *Romans 10:9, 10*—Confess, believe. *Romans 10:13*—Call upon the Lord.

7. *John 6:37*—Whoever comes to Him He will not cast out. *John 10:28*—He gives believers eternal life; they will never perish; no one can remove them from His hand. *1 John 2:25*—He has promised us eternal life. *1 John 5:14, 15*—When we ask anything according to His will, He hears and answers us.

8. *1 John 5:4, 5*—The person who believes by faith that Jesus is the Son of God overcomes the world. *Romans 8:37-39*—Through Christ, we are more than conquerors; nothing can separate us from God's love if we are "in Christ Jesus." *2 Peter 1:3*—When we know God, His power provides everything we need for life and godliness.

Section III—1. People seek success through accomplishments, education, popularity, beauty, wealth, position, and power. None of these things guarantee ultimate success and fulfillment. Although they may not be wrong in themselves (and may actually be used by God), one accomplishment can be "bettered" by another, education can become outdated, popularity can wane, beauty fade, wealth vanish, position and power crumble. Furthermore, these things have no value in the life that will come after death. When we receive Christ and establish Him as the foundation of our lives (for now and eternity), all those other things can be built on that foundation as God determines.

2. Personal answers.

3. Personal answers.

4. Personal answers.

LESSON 2

Section II—1. *Philippians 1:6*—God, Who chose us to be saved, will continue to work out His will in us until we are with Christ. *Philippians 2:12, 13*—As we work out our salvation, God will work in us both a desire and an ability to obey Him. (Note: We do not "work for" salvation. The phrase "work out" implies our endeavors to live for God after salvation.) *Philippians 3:12-14*—Christ chose us, and we press on to fulfill His purpose in choosing us. *Colossians 2:6, 7*—Christ wants us to walk (live) in Him, be rooted and built up in Him, and be established in the faith with thankfulness.

2. *Romans 7:18, 19*—The problem we face is "sin in the flesh," the sin still at work to rule over us and cause us to disobey God's will. *2 Corinthians 12:9*—Christ's grace and power are sufficient to overcome our weaknesses. *Galatians 2:20*—I must live by faith and die to self-effort. Christ lives out His life through me. *Ephesians 6:10, 11*—Our strength for living comes from God's power. In Him we can stand against the Devil. *Titus 2:11, 12*—The grace of God teaches us to deny ungodliness and worldly lusts and to live godly. *1 Peter 5:10*—The God of grace will perfect, establish, strengthen, and

settle us. *2 Peter 3:18*—We must grow in grace and the knowledge of Christ. *2 Peter 1:3, 4*—God's divine power, imparted to us, enables us to escape the pull of worldly lusts and to live godly lives. (Leader: Define "grace." [One possible definition is God's kind actions toward us through Christ.] Considering the problem presented in Romans 7, why is God's grace imperative to our growth in Christ?)

3. *John 14:23*—God and Christ dwell in each of us who belong to Him. *John 14:16, 17*—The Holy Spirit dwells in each believer.

4. *John 14:26*—He will teach us all things and bring them to our remembrance. *John 16:13*—He will guide us into all truth. *2 Corinthians 3:18*—We are being changed by the Spirit to reflect the Lord's glory. *Galatians 5:16-25*—The Spirit enables us to have victory over sin in the flesh. He produces godly virtues in us as we yield to His power. *Ephesians 3:16*—He strengthens us with God's power.

5. *Psalm 119:89, 160*—God's Word is true; it is settled forever in Heaven; it cannot be changed. *2 Timothy 3:16*—It is inspired by God. *2 Peter 1:20, 21*—The Scriptures are not a product of man's will or opinion; the writers were directed by the Holy Spirit.

6. *John 5:39*—To teach us of Christ and lead us to eternal life. *Romans 15:4*—For our learning, endurance, and comfort. *2 Timothy 3:15-17*—For wisdom leading to salvation; for doctrine (proper belief), reproof, correction, instruction in righteousness; for our maturity. *1 Peter 2:2*—For our growth. *Psalm 119:9*—For cleansing from sin as we pay attention to its words. (All our sins are forgiven by Christ's blood when we receive Him as Savior. Confessing our sin daily to God keeps an open relationship with our Heavenly Father. Obeying the Word through the Spirit will keep us from committing sin.) *Psalm 119:130*—For light and understanding.

7. *Hebrews 4:14-16*—We can bring our sins, weaknesses, and temptations to Christ and be assured of His understanding and enabling; through prayer we find mercy and grace to help us in our need. *1 John 5:14, 15*—We know He will answer any request in His will, especially if we are asking for spiritual growth in areas of our lives. *Philippians 4:6, 7*—We don't have to worry; God's peace will keep us. *Matthew 26:41*—We can pray that we will not give in to temptation.

8. *Acts 2:41-47*—A local church provides teaching in doctrine (v. 42), fellowship (v. 42), the administration of the two ordinances, baptism and the Lord's supper (vv. 41, 42), group prayer (v. 42), a group for meeting needs (vv. 44, 45), joint worship of God (v. 47). *Ephesians 4:11-16*—The church is a place where edification (building up) occurs as each person ministers to others. God expects each member to mature in faith and gain knowledge of Christ and doctrine.

9. *Hebrews 11:6*—Diligently seek Him. *Deuteronomy 4:29*—Seek Him wholeheartedly. *2 Timothy 2:15*—Be willing to study God's Word; desire to be prepared and fit for God's use. *2 Timothy 2:20, 21*—Keep yourself as a clean vessel so God can use you at any time. *2 Peter 3:13, 14*—Look forward to being united with Him, and be diligent to be found at peace with Him, spotless and blameless.

10. Personal answers. (Leader: Discuss the concept of "sacrifice" and what it means to be a "living sacrifice.")

Section III—1. Personal answers. (*Discuss:* What are some of the things Christians today are substituting for God's plan for growth? [Possible answers are things like reading devotional books, going to seminars, religious "busyness."] Although some of these things may not be bad in themselves, they may divert us from God's true means of spiritual progress.)

2. Personal answers. (Leader: Some ladies may find this question too personal to answer aloud. Others may be more willing. You could word the question, "What are some hindrances to spiritual growth?")

3. Personal answers. (Should be shared on a volunteer basis only.)

LESSON 3

Section II—1. *Isaiah 14:12-15*—Lucifer (Satan) desired to set himself up as God. *Genesis 3:1-6*—Satan, having rebelled against God, tempted Eve by planting thoughts of self-exaltation: "ye shall be as gods." *Daniel 4:28-37*—Nebuchadnezzar's heart was lifted up in pride as he surveyed the kingdom he had built. The Lord abased him for taking God's glory. (*Discuss:* How might we exhibit self-exaltation? Answers include being driven for recognition and honor, trusting in self and failing to seek God's guidance and help, manipulating and dominating others.)

2. *Isaiah 42:8*—God does not share His glory with any other. *Matthew 23:8-12*—We are to consider God and Christ our Master, and we are not to exalt ourselves.

3. (a) Korah challenged the position of leadership God gave Moses and Aaron and felt that he and others of his group had an equal right to rule. (b) Moses responded humbly. He fell on his face and left his defense in God's hands. (c) God showed His disapproval by judging Korah and those who rebelled with him. (*Discuss:* How does the extreme demand for rights today actually promote rebellion?)

4. *1 Samuel 15:22, 23*—Rebellion is equated with disobedience to God, witchcraft, iniquity, idolatry, rejecting God's Word. *Romans 13:2*—Rebellion is resisting the ordinance of God, the consequence of which is judgment.

5. (a) The younger son demanded his inheritance money; he wasted it on self-indulgent living. (After his crisis, he changed his attitude.) The older brother, although obedient, cared for neither his father nor his brother. His self-centered heart was resentful and unforgiving, and it's evident he was not working for his father out of love. He focused on what hadn't been done for him rather than on what he had (a loving father, good home, inheritance). (b) The father was loving, giving, forgiving, gentle, compassionate, and patient. He seemingly thought little about himself. (*Discuss:* If the father had been self-centered, how might he have acted in this account?)

6. (a) Eliab accused David of being proud, naughty, and nosey. (b) David was not guilty of any of these things. (c) Eliab, who was the oldest son, put down his youngest brother. (d) Eliab used criticism to attack David, perhaps because of his position as

oldest, his pride in being in Saul's army, or his jealousy of David's being anointed as king (1 Sam. 16:13). (e) Eliab didn't understand that David was obeying his father's instructions and carrying out God's will against the Philistines.

7. (a) The Pharisees accused the blind man of being an ignorant sinner. (b) The blind man had done nothing wrong. (c) They use intimidating questions, sarcasm, and insult. (d) They felt proud of their position and probably felt the conviction of sin in their hearts, which caused them to act with malice. (e) They lacked understanding about Jesus as God's Messiah.

8. (a) The disciples accused the woman of wasting money and not giving to the poor. (b) She was not doing wrong. (c) Their criticism is shown by murmuring and complaining, perhaps in a "gossipy" way. (d) Perhaps they wanted to seem super-spiritual or were pricked in their hearts by her loving worship of their Master. (e) They did not understand the importance of worshiping God's Son. (*Discuss:* In some situations, the person the faultfinder is criticizing may be guilty of a fault. Does this justify the critic's hurtful words? Does this mean we should never confront a person's sin? How should we handle people's faults? [See, for instance, Galatians 6:1.])

9. *Proverbs 3:5-9*—We must trust totally in the Lord and not in ourselves, acknowledge Him in every area of life and seek His will, fear the Lord and honor Him even with material possessions. *Psalm 34:1-3*—We must give praise and honor, not to ourselves, but to God. *1 Corinthians 6:20*—We belong to God and are to glorify Him in our bodies and spirits. (*Discuss:* Are any forms of pride "acceptable"? How can we handle the praise of others?)

10. *Romans 13:1*—Be subject. *1 Peter 2:13-17*—We are to submit to them for the Lord's sake.

11. (a) Phrases that relate to our problem with self-centeredness are "let nothing be done through strife or vainglory"; "esteem other better than themselves"; "look not every man on his own things." (b) As our model of humility, Christ made Himself of no reputation, took the place of a servant, humbled Himself to God's will, did not grasp at "rights." He laid aside His glory, and rather than focus on self, He focused on the needs of others. God then exalted Him. (*Discuss:* What are some practical ways we can put off self-centeredness?)

12. That which comes out of our mouths should be good for building up others (not ourselves) and ministering grace (loving-kindness) to those who hear it.

13. A thought that has helped me in many situations in which I could have "reacted" is that if I react with a proud heart, God will then resist rather than help me. If, however, I respond humbly (in word, attitude, etc.), God will give me grace. I don't want to "cut off" God's grace that helps in any situation. Therefore, the answer could be, When you are proud, God "resists" you (or opposes you); when you are humble, He grants grace to help you in that situation.

Section III—1. Our sense of worth comes from the understanding that God created us, sought us, redeemed us, loves us, sanctifies us, equips and uses us. Abasing ourselves simply means we recognize our rightful place under God's power and for His work. Even though we are sinners, God graciously grants us the feeling of "satisfaction" (a better word, I think, than pride) in bearing fruit for Him.

2. Personal answers.

3. Repent and confess the sin to God; ask forgiveness of anyone you have offended, if needed. Perhaps you should ask yourself, "Why did I think/say/do that?" Ask the Lord to point out wrong ideas and work out the humility of Christ in your life by His grace. Seek to respond humbly in testing situations.

LESSON 4

Section II—1. (a) It flowed with milk and honey; it had bountiful fruit; it was an exceedingly good land. (b) The people were strong; there were walled cities; it was surrounded by great nations on all sides; there were giants.

2. The Israelites would not be able to take the land.

3. Joshua and Caleb wanted to go at once. They felt they could conquer the inhabitants. They trusted God to enable them to win.

4. Fear; comparison of themselves with others; focus on their own inadequacies; disregard of God's character and promises (unbelief).

5. They started to accuse God of evil.

6. The ten spies were basically saying, "We're nobody!" The Israelites began to feel sorry for themselves, stating, "We're better off dead"; "God's not treating us right"; and "Let's go back to Egypt."

7. They were looking at the situation in light of God's presence, power, and promises. They did not look at the Israelites' weaknesses or the land's obstacles but on God's ability.

8. Their discouragement led to disobedience to God's will, loss of blessing, and God's chastening.

9. Both Joshua and Caleb were allowed to enter and possess the Land of Promise.

10. (Leader: Summarize the events of chapter 18 for your group in order to help ladies who lack a Biblical background.) Elijah felt like he wanted to die; he felt that he was a failure (v. 4); he was overwhelmed by the wickedness of the king, queen, and God's people (vv. 10, 14); he saw himself as being utterly alone and helpless; he spoke as if the situation were hopeless; he felt as if his zeal for the Lord had been for nothing.

11. A very real threat on his life; weariness; hunger; the spiritual apostasy of his people; perhaps a lack of human fellowship and encouragement.

12. The Lord fed him and let him rest.

13. The Lord spoke to him (v. 9); the Lord asked him probing questions so that Elijah could examine his feelings and actions; the Lord reminded Elijah of His presence and power (vv. 11-13); He revealed His plan to him (vv. 15-17); He corrected Elijah's faulty thinking that he alone was faithful to God (v. 18); He provided Elijah with a human companion for fellowship and support (v. 19).

14. *Daniel*—(a) Daniel read the Word of God for insight (v. 2); then he prayed, confessing sin, exalting God, and asking God to restore Israel. (b) God sent an angelic messenger to assure Daniel of God's sovereign care over His people. *Hannah*—(a) Hannah also prayed, speaking honestly to God and presenting her request. She left her cares with God, trusting Him, and she "went her way, and did eat, and her countenance was no more sad" (v. 18). (b) God answered her prayers. *Paul and Silas*—(a) Paul and Silas prayed and sang praises to God. (b) God sent supernatural help to release them from bondage. They were able to witness of Christ even in their hardship; as a result, the jailer and his family received Christ. (*Discuss:* What do we learn about dealing with discouragement from these three cases?)

15. (Ask volunteers to share their answers. Psalms 34 and 37 and Isaiah 40 are three possible passages.)

Section III—1. We can always find people who are more productive or less productive than ourselves. I need to focus on God's plan for me. If someone seems more spiritual and fruitful, I may begin to think, "What's the use?" and slack off. Also, when I look at my own failures and weaknesses, I discount God's grace to work in me and through me. It is never I, but Christ. (See Galatians 2:20 and Ephesians 3:20.)

2. Exodus 4:10-12; Judges 6:11-16; Romans 12:3-8; 1 Corinthians 12:13-25; 2 Corinthians 10:12.

3. "Examining ourselves" is searching our hearts for sin that needs to be confessed (1 Cor. 11:28-31). If we have sinned, we confess it to God (1 John 1:9); then we go on in the joy and freedom we have through Christ's blood. This is different from a person's continually thinking about how she has failed God or can't serve God because she's not talented enough. Such a person is mired in self-pity and will not be spiritually fruitful. These thoughts are Biblically wrong and are chains of Satan.

4. Such a philosophy can lead to frustration or, at worst, self-destruction! Although it is not unbiblical to set goals and work hard to obtain them, we need to have an understanding of our human limitations. Some handicaps and lack of ability can be rectified, but some cannot. A person who can't sing on key will never become a great opera singer. As a Christian I might say, "God will enable me to do whatever is within His will for me."

5. Look to God's power to do whatever He calls us to do. Possible references include Philippians 4:11-13; 2 Corinthians 3:5; 9:8; 12:9, 10.

6. We may think, "God is punishing me," or "God is unfair."

7. There's the "good old days" mentality. We idealize the past and forget its troubles. (The Israelites did this in Exodus 16:2 and 3.) We may also think that "the grass is greener on the other side." We look at other people and assert that their lives are better than ours. Then there is the "if only" syndrome. We think we would be happy "if only" this or that would happen. (We will deal with this in lesson 8.)

8. (a) Physical factors can greatly affect our emotional state. If we are burned out physically, we are usually burned out emotionally. The remedy is extended rest and

relaxation (reduce that schedule!) and alteration of diet to meet the nutritional needs of life's demands. (*Discuss:* Prolonged physical illness can also cause discouragement. How can a Christian deal with such a situation in her life?) (b) When we dwell on the evil and ungodliness of society, we begin to feel that the world is out of control. We should limit our exposure to television and news programs; be in God's Word to remind ourselves of God's sovereign control of all things. (Read Isaiah 40!) (c) Elijah, for example, felt, "I'm the only one." God reminded him that other people were still faithful to God, and He also provided Elisha to be a personal encourager to Elijah. We need godly friends and strong Christian fellowship, especially in a local church setting. (d) Again, continued stress wears us out emotionally. The angel told Elijah, "The journey is too great for thee." In Nehemiah 4:10 the Israelites became discouraged by the immensity of the task of rebuilding the city wall. At such times in our lives, we must focus on life's priorities, being sure not to neglect our spiritual relationship to God. Then we may have to let go of control (as Moses did), trust God for what we can't do, and delegate to others as we can. (*Discuss:* Elijah also experienced discouragement because of the Jews' spiritual failure and sin. How can the failings of other people cause us to be discouraged? Other than faulty thinking, were the causes of Elijah's feelings his "fault"?)

9. Personal answers.

10. It helps us focus on God rather than ourselves; it helps us realize there is a solution, known to God. Honest examination enables us to confess sin that may be causing discouragement.

11. Again, it shifts our focus to God. We meditate on His attributes that are the source of help in trouble.

12. When we are stuck in the "slimy pit" of circumstances or our own emotions, the unchanging facts of God's Word enable us to get a firm footing. Once our thoughts become settled, our emotions will follow. Our "goings" will be "established," and praise will be in our hearts and on our lips (Ps. 40:2, 3).

LESSON 5

Section II—1. God is the ruler of the earth. Those who reject His rule will submit, either willingly or unwillingly. (They shall be broken with a rod of iron [v. 9].)

2. *Luke 12:4, 5*—Fear of God will cause us to turn to God and avoid Hell. *Proverbs 8:13*—Fear of the Lord causes us to hate what is evil. *2 Corinthians 5:9-11*—A "fear" of giving an account to Christ of how we have lived will motivate us to faithfully labor. Also, recognizing that unbelievers must face His wrath in judgment, we witness to them. *Hebrews 12:28*—We avail ourselves of His grace so that we may serve Him acceptably.

3. *Exodus 34:6, 7*—Merciful, gracious, long-suffering, abundant in goodness and truth, forgiving. *Psalm 25:6-10*—Tender in mercies and loving-kindness, merciful, good, upright, teaching and guiding the meek. *Psalm 145:8, 9*—Gracious, full of

compassion, slow to anger, of great mercy, shows goodness and mercies to all. *Hebrews 4:15, 16*—Sympathetic to our struggles, gracious, merciful, willing to help us in our need.

4. *Romans 8:15, 16*—We do not need to live in fearfulness of God as slaves who will be beaten, but we may think of Him as a loving father who cares for us. *1 John 4:16-19*—God perfectly loves us. This removes the fear of being judged and of God's making bad things happen to us if we commit a sin. (Our sins were judged at the cross and covered by Christ's blood. We need to practice 1 John 1:9 to restore our fellowship with our Heavenly Father.)

5. *Psalm 31:19*—Great is His goodness toward those who fear Him. *Psalm 103:1-5*—These benefits are listed for His people: heals diseases, redeems us from destruction, crowns us with loving-kindness and mercy, satisfies us with good things so that we are renewed. *Romans 8:31-39*—God is for us. In Christ, He freely gives us all good things. No one can condemn us. Nothing can separate us from His love.

6. *Proverbs 3:11, 12*—God loves and delights in us. He therefore chastens and corrects us when He must. I should not despise His chastening (or Him) or be weary of it. *Psalm 103:8-14*—He is merciful, gracious, slow to anger, does not always scold, nor does He keep on being angry. He does not deal with us as our sins deserve. He pities us and knows our frailty. It is implied through this that He practices great forbearance in dealing with us, and when we confess our sins, He removes them far away from us. I should honor God and confess my sins quickly. *1 John 1:5—2:1*—God is light. He is faithful and just (fair) to us; He will cleanse us from all unrighteousness when we confess; He has provided an Advocate for us. I must not lie or deceive myself about my own spiritual condition. I must confess all sin and be cleansed.

7. (a) Discipline will most likely come when we have repeatedly ignored the conviction of His Spirit, refusing to repent and continuing to sin (also called "hardening the heart"). (b) Not every bad thing is chastisement from God. Some things allow the glory of God to be revealed in the situation (e.g., John 9:3); some are spiritual tests meant to strengthen us (James 1:2, 3).

8. *Psalm 23:1-4; Isaiah 40:11*—God is a loving, kind shepherd, caring gently for all the needs of His sheep (us!). *Psalm 91:4*—He is pictured as a mother bird who protects her young ones by covering them with her wings. *Psalm 103:13, 14*—God is compared to a father who understands his children, their weaknesses and limitations. *Matthew 7:7-11*—Again, God is like a father who would respond kindly to his son. He longs to do good to his children. In each of these "pictures" God is the more powerful figure presented, while we, as sheep, young birds, or children, are weak and needy and totally dependent.

9. *Luke 8:43-48*—Her need was physical in nature. She was timid to approach Christ and fearful of His reaction. He comforted her, encouraged her, and blessed her. *John 8:3-11*—Her need was spiritual; she needed to be forgiven and to establish a right relationship to God. The passage does not mention her reaction, but surely she must

have been humiliated and terrified in facing stoning; Christ forgave her and set her on God's path for her.

Section III—1. The child should fear the father's position of authority and honor, the fact that the father will discipline him/her for disobedience, perhaps even the father's physical superiority.

2. The child should not have to fear that the father will harm, neglect, or reject her. Harm destroys trust. Even with a proper fear, the child will trust in the father's expressed, unconditional love.

3. A perfect father would encourage, care, comfort, instruct, meet needs. This would cause the child to love and rely on her father.

4. An understanding father would not become angry with a child who simply was unable to do what was asked or could not do it perfectly. A patient father is satisfied when the child's intent is to obey even if her efforts are clumsy and imperfect. If a child deliberately and repeatedly disobeyed the father's directions, the father would have to discipline for the best interests of the child.

5. He wants his child to grow up properly and to be healthy.

6. The discipline would be fair and just; it would fit the disobedience. It would break the will, not the spirit, and lead to the child's repentance.

7. The loving relationship between the father and child would be intimate. They would spend time together and talk. The child would love, respect, and trust the father. The father would listen, care, help, and encourage.

8. His goal always is for the child to become all the good things she was meant to become.

9. Personal answers.

10. (a) Possible answers include a poor relationship with her own father; overly sensitive conscience; ignorance of Scriptural view of God; dwelling on her own failures and sin rather than putting them "under the blood" by faith; listening to the lies of Satan; comparison of self with others. (b) Correction comes by a deeper knowledge of God through Scriptures.

11. (a) We may mentally overemphasize the verses that reflect God's judgment of sin. To counterbalance, understand His full acceptance of us in Christ Jesus (Eph. 1:4-6). We need to realize that even though we are sinners, when we are filled with the Spirit and generally living obediently to God's Word, we can please God. (See 1 Thessalonians 4:1; Hebrews 13:16; 1 John 3:22.) (b) With regard to our sinning, we have already seen that God is very merciful and slow to anger in dealing with us. God does not "punish" us, but He may discipline us if we harden our hearts over a long stretch of continued sin. (c) Another lie of Satan, first used in the Garden of Eden on Eve, is that God is really holding out on us and doesn't want to give us what will make us happy. (Will everything we want make us happy?) The Bible declares that God truly longs to give His children good gifts when they are within His will (e.g., Psalm 37:3-5; Matthew 7:11). (d) Things going wrong don't always indicate God's chastening us.

In general, life is full of irritations and problems. God may use these to teach us spiritual truth even when we are in fellowship with Him. (*Discuss:* Why do people blame God when things go wrong? Who else might they blame?) (e) Again, Satan wants us to withhold our lives from God so that we will not be fully controlled by the Spirit. Some people are afraid that God would send them to a foreign country if they gave Him control of their lives. But when we yield to God totally, He works in our desires so that doing His will brings great joy (Phil. 2:13). A life given over to God's control, even with trials, is the most joyful, satisfying life (see Psalm 16).

LESSON 6

Section II—1. (a) A sudden storm put them in danger. (b) Christ was not troubled; He was asleep in the boat. (c) The disciples had to tell Jesus their need. (d) He rebuked them for their fear and lack of faith. (e) They had proper fear of Christ as God, as opposed to fearfulness of the storm. (*Discuss:* Does the Lord always take care of our problems immediately? See 1 Peter 5:10.)

2. (a) They were to be strong and courageous (vv. 6, 9) and determined to obey God (v. 7). (b) They were to do what God commanded, to think on His words, and to prepare to carry out their responsibilities (v. 11). (c) God's assurance was He would be with them and not fail them and they would succeed.

3. *Psalm 34:19*—The Lord will deliver me out of all my afflictions (as He chooses!) *Isaiah 41:10*—I am not to fear, for God will help and uphold me in all circumstances. *Philippians 4:19*—God shall supply all my needs. *1 John 5:14, 15*—God will answer all my prayers within His will.

4. "Fear of man" is a snare that can entangle us. (Sometimes we may fear what others may do to us, but we probably fear more often what they think of us.) If we let this become an influencing factor, we may step out of line with God's will for us.

5. God made Saul king, but he began to worry about keeping his position. Because he tried to secure his kingship rather than trusting God, he began to fret about the people's opinion of him. (See also 1 Samuel 18:6-8.) He failed to obey God totally because he didn't want to displease the people. God took the kingdom from him because of this disobedience.

6. Do not put expectations upon people, but upon God. When we trust totally in God, we will not be moved by fear. The opinions of people are vanity, as are the influences people may seek to exert upon us (wealth, social position, oppression). God's power, mercy, and justice are our hope. (*Discuss:* Does this indicate that we should not ask the opinions of others about life's matters? How is this different from "fear of man"?)

7. *Fear:* Moses was not eloquent but slow of speech. *Solution:* God, Who made Moses' tongue, would enable him to say what was necessary.

8. *Fear:* Gideon was a nobody. (He had no credentials!) *Solution:* In God's eyes, Gideon was a man of valor, and He would be with him. (God was Gideon's credential!)

9. *Fear:* Paul's human weakness to do God's work in his own power. *Solution:* Preach the gospel (God's Word has power) and be filled with the Spirit's power.

10. *Matthew 6:31-34*—Seek God first; trust Him for our needs; don't worry. *Philippians 4:6-8:* Pray; present our requests with thanksgiving; let God's peace rule our minds as we focus on thinking right. *1 Peter 5:7*—Cast our cares on God. *Isaiah 26:3*—Keep our thoughts on God. *Psalm 42:5-8*—Hope in God; remember God; trust in His loving-kindness and His answering of prayer.

11. *Martha*—(a) In attitude she was "cumbered" (we'd say stressed out!); in action she was frantically busy. (b) She was worried about her household and supper chores. (c) She was fearful (v. 41) that everything wouldn't get done or done to perfection, which would actually be pride. (d) Her fear caused self-pity and criticism against Jesus and Mary. (e) Personal answers. *Mary*—(a) She desired to hear God's words; her actions were quiet and calm. (b) Though it could seem she was lazy or thoughtless, she was simply putting spiritual priorities over food. (c) Her actions were caused by a deep reverence and love for Christ and a spiritual hunger in her soul. *Jesus*—(a) He rebuked Martha for being burdened, worried, and troubled. (b) He commended Mary for making a choice for that which was useful, or beneficial. (c) He rebuked Martha because she chose to be controlled by her feelings of worry regarding material things. (d) He commended Mary for her spiritual priority. The Lord would have been content with a quality visit with the sisters, followed by a light lunch of leftovers! (*Discuss:* Does this account teach neglect of responsibilities? What does it teach us? How might Martha and Mary's story be applied to what goes on in our local churches?)

12. God's power, which can work in any situation, is also working in us; love that keeps on loving others in any circumstance; self-control to think right thoughts when tempted to fear.

Section III—1. We may turn to other people; do activities to mask our fears (eating, shopping, watching television); put our trust in lotteries or horoscopes.

2. We must turn to Him, pray honestly, get into His Word, keep our minds on Him. We may ask others to pray. Finally, if God—or sanctified common sense—leads us to take an action, take it!

3. (a) Fears can eat away at us and cause us to step out of God's will, as Saul did. (b) Fear can lead to disobedience, lying, cheating, stealing, jealousy, anger, hatred, depression, and more. (c) It can cause stress-related illnesses, such as stomach problems, headaches, high blood pressure, back pain, and more.

4. Personal answers. (Leader: Answers should be shared on a volunteer basis only.)

5. Don't know enough; too shy; never tried it.

6. It may be God's will for us to do a certain work, but our fear causes refusal to obey. God's work done in His power is often a joy to our hearts as we meet people's needs.

7. We must focus on God's power as our source of strength and ability. Possible

verses include Philippians 4:13; 2 Corinthians 9:8; 12:9, 10. (*Discuss:* Does this mean we ought to do everything we're asked to do? How can you discern God's desire for you? [Hint: Determine if your refusal is based on fear.])

8. Confess your sin (1 John 1:9).

9. Personal answers.

LESSON 7

Section II—1. (a) We are to put all bitterness away from us. (b) We grieve the Holy Spirit because of our sin. (c) Kindness, tenderheartedness, a forgiving spirit. (d) The motivation is Christ's forgiveness of us, His willingness to love us when we had sinned against Him, and our goal to be like God. (*Discuss:* In verse 31 bitterness, wrath, anger, clamor, and evil speaking are all mentioned together. Are these sins related? Explain your answer.)

2. (a) "Bitterness" is paired up with "envy" and "strife." (The Greek word for "envy" means "jealousy of another's goodness and desire to cause it trouble." The Greek word for "strife" means "selfishness and self-will.") (b) We are not to glory about it (boast or exult) and not to lie about it. (*Discuss:* How might a person who is bitter do either of these things?) (c) This behavior is described as earthly, sensual (carnal), and devilish. (d) It produces confusion and every evil work. (Leader: If it is relevant to your group, discuss how such bitterness [as described in James] affects a local church body.)

3. (a) Bitterness troubles and defiles a person. When a woman is bitter, her mind is controlled by the person or event that caused her anger. She has no mental or emotional peace because of it. Bitterness also leads to spiritual defilement, or the stain of sin on her heart. (b) Follow peace and holiness and watch diligently to keep ourselves in the grace of God. (*Discuss:* How can a woman do these things?)

4. *Genesis 25:28-34; 27:6-45*—Jacob craftily obtained Esau's birthright (position of authority as eldest son and double share of the inheritance) and blessing. Esau's bitterness led him to want to kill his brother. *Genesis 37:3-28*—Joseph's brothers became bitter because of their father's partiality and Joseph's seemingly "egotistical" dreams. They sold him into slavery. *Esther 3:1-6; 5:9-14*—Haman became bitter because Mordecai would not bow down to him and honor him. Haman could not enjoy his position, but plotted to kill Mordecai. This plot led to his own death.

5. Joseph saw God's hand in the situation. God worked through the evil actions of the brothers to produce ultimate good. Joseph forgave his brothers and did good to them.

6. *Luke 17:3, 4*—We must forgive as many times as is necessary. *Colossians 3:12-14*—We are to be forbearing and forgiving, even as Christ was.

7. *Leviticus 19:18*—Do not hold a grudge or seek revenge, but rather love others as yourself. *Proverbs 20:22*—Don't repay evil for evil; wait upon the Lord to take care of your situation. *Matthew 5:44-46*—We are to love, bless, do good to, and pray for

those who have treated us poorly. (*Discuss:* Must we forgive if the person does not repent of the wrong he or she has done to us? If the person does not repent, where does that leave us with our anger?)

8. *Romans 8:28*—God will use all things in our lives to produce good for us. *Psalm 37:1-9*—When we commit ourselves to God, He will establish us and bless us.

9. (a) He was envious of the prosperity of the wicked. (b) His bitterness had caused deep pain, spiritual decline, and a feeling that his obedience to God had been in vain. (c) He was delivered from his bitterness as he focused on the sovereignty and eventual justice of God (vv. 17-20) and as he saw himself as the object of God's love and grace.

Section III—1. Signs of bitterness could be "touchy" anger, sarcasm, complaining, a critical attitude, depression, self-pity, or restless activity.

2. Pride, revenge, desire to control, stubbornness, enjoyment of our anger (which is really in control).

3. We are to forgive as God forgave us; our lives are to be characterized by love and holiness; God will judge us on how we lived as believers; Christ bought us with His blood, and we are not free to do as we please, but we must please Him.

4. Possible answers include Ephesians 4:32; Philippians 4:13; 2 Timothy 2:24; Matthew 5:44.

5. If a person who has offended is a believer and his or her sin is affecting the work of God, then the person should be lovingly confronted. (Matthew 18 is in a local church context.) But let us always be sure the offense is not petty. (*Discuss:* In a local church why is it important to confront a person who is sinning?) It would also be important to "clear the air" in the circle of our immediate family. Bitterness should never take root between spouses or parents and children. If the offender is an unbeliever, you could try to discuss the issue, but since that one is not of God's family, don't expect him or her to respond Biblically. If he or she does not apologize, you must forgive anyway. Finally, there are times when an offense has taken place in your heart and mind, and the matter can be settled between you and God. In such cases, you might do more damage by telling someone she offended you if she wasn't even aware of it! Then that person might begin to feel resentment.

6. (a) Be diligent to watch for bitterness (Heb. 12:15). (b) If an offense occurs, forgive based on God's command in Scripture (Matt. 6:14, 15). (c) Confess any wrong reactions: pride, words, etc. (1 John 1:9). (d) Talk to the offender, if necessary (Matt. 18:15). (e) If feelings of resentment or thoughts of the offense resurface, go to God in prayer. Restate your forgiveness, resist Satan's attack, think on what is good, be filled with the Spirit (James 4:7; Phil. 4:8; Gal. 5:16).

LESSON 8

Section II—1. Not glorifying (recognizing, honoring) God and not being thankful.

2. They lead to a vain imagination (wrong thinking), a darkened heart (unguided

morals), professing wisdom but being foolish (self-deceived), worshiping idols (putting other things in God's place). (*Discuss:* These four descending steps describe unbelievers. Would the pattern be similar in the life of a believer who stops honoring God and being thankful? How would it be the same? different? Remember that thoughts determine attitudes, words, and actions.)

3. Man's desire is never satisfied by the material and temporal; seeking after "things" is vanity (emptiness).

4. Ungodly attitudes and behavior; strife; wrong praying.

5. *Proverbs 15:16*—A person who follows the Lord and yet has little wealth is better off than one who has much without the Lord. *Proverbs 16:8*—Righteousness is better than riches. *Philippians 4:11-13*—Through Christ, we can learn to be content in all of life's situations. *1 Timothy 6:6-8*—Godliness is the believer's goal, not wealth. We can't take riches to Heaven. Be content with food and clothing (most basic needs). *Hebrews 13:5*—Be content with what we have, which is God! (*Discuss:* In what ways does our culture aim at making us discontent? How can we avoid the world's "snares" of covetousness in very practical terms? [Suggestions include throw out junk mail catalogs; limit window-shopping; don't misuse credit cards.])

6. *Genesis 15, 16, 21*—God promised Abram and Sarai, who was barren, an heir. They would not wait for God to bring it about, so they planned to produce an heir through Sarai's maid (who would act as a surrogate mother). When the maid conceived, Sarai became jealous, quarreled with her husband, and dealt harshly with the maid. When Abram and Sarai later had their own son, this maid's child caused rivalry and contention. *1 Samuel 8*—The Israelites grew discontent with God's ruling over them. They came and demanded a king like the other nations had. In so doing, they rejected God and His will for them at that time (v. 7). They would have to give of their material possessions and households to meet the king's needs. *1 Kings 21*—King Ahab set his desires on a man's vineyard (part of the man's inheritance). Ahab allowed his wicked wife to kill the man and gain the land. God told Ahab that evil would come upon him and his family and that he would die a bitter death.

7. *Psalm 37:3-7*—We are to trust, do good, delight ourselves in the Lord, commit our way to the Lord, rest in the Lord, wait patiently, not fret. *Psalm 62:5*—Wait upon God; put our expectations on Him. *Psalm 130:5*—Wait for the Lord; put hope in His Word. (*Discuss:* How can we be sure God will answer our prayers? What if He says no?)

8. (a) Some examples are Hannah, Abraham, David, Daniel, and Joseph. (b) Abraham offered sacrifices to God; the others gave verbal praise.

9. (a) The incident demonstrates our tendency to be selfish and unthankful. (b) The Samaritan truly understood God's goodness in healing him, and as a result he worshiped Christ and thanked Him. He had faith. (*Discuss:* What would you think to be the spiritual condition of the nine lepers from this point on? What about the Samaritan?)

10. *1 Chronicles 16:29*—When we are grateful, we will give glory to God and

worship Him in holiness. We will bring offerings to Him. (*Discuss:* What are the "offerings" we can bring to God?) *Psalm 5:11*—We will rejoice and be joyful. *Psalm 104:33, 34*—We will sing unto the Lord; we will be glad and meditate on Him. (*Discuss:* What is the relationship between meditating on God and being thankful?) *Hebrews 13:15*—We will praise God and give thanks.

11. *Colossians 1:9-12*—As Paul prayed for the Colossians' spiritual growth, he prayed that they would give thanks to God (v. 12). *Colossians 2:6, 7*—As they were growing in the faith, they were to abound in thanksgiving. *Colossians 3:15-17*—Giving thanks is mentioned twice in this passage, along with allowing the Word to dwell in us and praise to come from us. *Colossians 4:2*—As we pray, we will express thanksgiving.

12. Giving thanks is an indication of a Spirit-filled life.

Section III—1. When we are thankful, we focus on God, and we want to know Him more. We honor Him and recognize Him as God, the Giver of all we have (Rom. 1:21). When we stop being thankful, we become disgruntled with Him and the life He has given us. We scorn His grace and mercy and move away from Him in our hearts.

2. Answers include grumbling, complaining, criticizing, self-pity, covetousness, greed, selfishness.

3. Marriage, money, prestige, things, a change in other people. These can all fade away. Only Christ is the same yesterday, today, forever.

4. God may make us wait to test obedience, to strengthen our faith, to purify sinful attitudes or motives. Perhaps He is working in someone else's life in answer to our prayers. Possible verses include Psalm 27:14; 1 Peter 5:10; 2 Corinthians 12:9, 10. (*Discuss:* Not all praying is Biblical. How might people "pray and wait" when they already have God's answer? Other instances when "pray and wait" is not using sanctified common sense include health problems or a physically abusive marriage. In these cases, seek help!)

5. (a) We are trying to take God's place. (b) It will destroy gratitude because God has not done the work, but we ourselves. (c) Waiting for God develops patience, faith, peace.

6. Personal answers. (Leader: The answers to questions 6-8 are personal and should not be shared with the group. However, you may reword these questions for group discussion; e.g., What kinds of things cause us to be discontent?)

7. Personal answers.

8. Personal answers.

9. Thank God in prayer; praise Him in song; give glory to Him verbally; meditate on His Word and His works.

10. Joy, peace, love for God, desire to serve Him, a more meaningful spiritual life.

LESSON 9

Section II—1. Love not the world or the things of the world. The Greek word for love, *agapao*, indicates a direction of the will and finding one's joy in something.

2. The love of the Father will not be in us.

3. The lust of the flesh, the lust of the eyes, the pride of life.

4. It and all it contains are transient. We would be setting our love on a vapor that will disappear. But our love and obedience to God have eternal results.

5. (a) The fruit was good for food (but so was all the other fruit in the garden). (b) The fruit was pleasant to the eye, enticing. (c) It would make Adam and Eve as gods, knowing good and evil. (*Discuss:* How did Satan twist words in tempting Eve? Does he use the same tactic today? How?)

6. (a) David was enticed by the lust of the eye and the lust of the flesh. (b) Uriah persisted in practicing self-control because it was the proper thing to do. In contrast, David went to great lengths to carry out his sin! (*Discuss:* How could David have responded when he saw Bathsheba that would have kept him in line with God's will?)

7. (a) The pride of life. (b) Evidently, these envoys were "big shots." He wanted to impress them with his kingdom and power. Perhaps he hoped to avoid war by this display rather than trusting God.

8. *Proverbs 11:4*—Riches cannot save our souls; only God's righteousness can do that. *Proverbs 23:5*—Worldly wealth is unstable and can suddenly disappear. *Luke 12:34*—That which you "treasure" has hold on your heart.

9. *Deuteronomy 8:11-14*—Prosperity causes us to forget God and inflates our pride. (This relates to thankfulness in lesson 8.) *Matthew 13:22*—Worldly attraction and deceitful riches choke out God's Word and make us unfruitful Christians. *Luke 12:15-21*—A person can be so preoccupied with worldly success that he or she neglects the soul and salvation. *1 Timothy 6:9, 10*—The desire to become rich leads to temptations and snares and wrong desires; the love of money is a root of all kinds of evil that may lead us to spiritual downfall and much sorrow.

10. *Matthew 6:24*—A person cannot serve and be loyal to two masters. God wants our undivided loyalty and love. *John 15:19*—We are not of this world; the world is our enemy. *James 4:4*—A believer who is friendly toward the world is acting as an enemy of God as well as a spiritual adulterer. *1 Peter 2:9-11*—We have been chosen by God and, therefore, must be distinctly different from unbelievers. We are to be holiness and light, pilgrims and strangers on the earth. Fleshly lusts war against the soul.

11. *Abram*—Abram refused to take a reward lest it in any way dishonor the Lord and cast a doubt that God was his complete provider. (*Discuss:* How might we apply this principle to ourselves today? What temptations does the world offer to "get rich quick"? See Proverbs 13:11; 28:22.) *Daniel*—Daniel refused the gifts of the wicked king. Instead, he carried out his work as God's messenger. *Paul*—Paul considered every "pride of life" to be garbage and viewed every offering of the world as worthless compared to growing in his knowledge of Christ. (*Discuss:* Was Paul a fanatic, or do we need more of this desire among believers today? How can we cultivate the kind of spirit Paul had?) *Moses*—Moses could have been considered Pharaoh's son (pride of

life). He could have enjoyed all the pleasures of Egypt (lust of the flesh and eyes). But he chose to follow God and suffer for Him.

12. He chose to pitch his tent toward the wicked city of Sodom.

13. In the city of Sodom. (Note Lot's position; sitting at the city gate indicates that he was a city leader.)

14. Although Lot recognized God's mercy toward him, his love of Sodom's comforts caused him to linger (v. 16) even though he was on the brink of destruction. He also begged to be allowed to go to another city.

15. Lot, who was a "just man" (indicates he was a believer in God), was vexing his soul by his intimate association with ungodly culture.

16. *Luke 12:29-31*—Don't spend your life seeking after things; seek God's kingdom. *Romans 12:1, 2*—Give yourself completely over to God as a living sacrifice; do not be pressed into the mold of the world; be changed by the renewing of your mind so you can discern God's will. *2 Timothy 2:4*—Don't be entangled with this present life, but live to please God, Who has chosen you. *Titus 2:11-13*—The grace of God teaches us that we should deny ungodly lusts and live righteously as we anticipate the Savior's coming.

17. Be filled with and led by the Spirit.

18. He has blessed us with spiritual blessings; chosen us; made us holy and without blame before Him; adopted us; made us accepted in the Beloved; provided redemption through His blood; forgiven our sins; made known to us His will; given us an inheritance; sealed us with the Spirit; guaranteed a future hope.

19. God is great, and everything in Heaven and earth is His to give. He will provide all we need. Therefore we should thank and praise Him.

Section III—1. Personal answers.

2. (a) Food; alcohol; drugs; immoral sex; pornography; sexually oriented movies, television programs, and books. (b) Clothes; houses; household items; "things" of all kinds; cars; jewelry. (c) Possessions; career; education; achievements; beauty; popularity; money; wealth.

3. Money and possessions are "loaned" to us by God to use, and we may enjoy them, but our grasp on them should be very loose; neither should they take control of our hearts. They are not to become our god or an idol we worship. All that we have and use is for God's glory.

4. "Myself" is usually the first on our lists! (Leader: To discuss in a group setting, you may ask, "What are some of the things that we consider important in our lives? In the next lesson, we will discuss what to do when something in our lives becomes an idol.)

5. Continue to practice a thankful attitude toward all that God has done for us in Christ. Meditate on spiritual things. (Remember, we think about what is important to us!) Keep an eternal perspective—what will last is that which has eternal value.

6. *Lust of the Flesh*—Avoid: Reading and watching things that cause impure

thoughts; uncontrolled eating; tobacco, alcohol, drugs; immodest behavior and dress. Cultivate: Purity; modesty; self-control. *Lust of the Eyes*—Avoid: Overemphasis on shopping and use of credit; mail-order catalogs; TV and Web shopping sprees. Cultivate: Contentment (make do with what you have if it's sufficient); thankfulness; self-control. *Pride of Life*—Avoid: Unhealthy emphasis on career, goals, education. About any endeavor, ask: Is this drawing me closer to God? Cultivate: Humility and a desire for the honor that comes from God.

7. Personal answers.

LESSON 10

Section II—1. *Genesis 35:1-4*—Jacob recognized that before he could worship God, he and his family were responsible to get rid of any other gods in whom they were trusting. *Joshua 24:14, 15*—In order to serve God in sincerity and truth, we must remove other gods from our lives. We must choose to serve God alone. *1 Samuel 7:3, 4*—In order to "return to God," it is necessary to put away other gods and seek to please Him first. (*Discuss:* In each of these instances, what would have been the spiritual result if the people had refused to obey?)

2. *Exodus 20:2-5*—We are not to serve any god or thing except God. *Mark 12:30*—We are to love God with all our hearts, souls, minds, and strength. *Romans 6:16-18*—We become servants to anything by which we are controlled. We are not to be servants of sin. *1 Corinthians 6:12*—Even though something may not be harmful or evil, we are not to be under the power (control) of anything. *Hebrews 12:1*—We are instructed to put aside every "weight" (encumbrance) and every sin that keeps us from spiritual progress.

3. Our hearts are deceived. We think that the idol will meet the emotional needs that we have. But only God can provide all we need.

4. It hinders our fellowship with our Heavenly Father.

5. *Psalm 90:8*—God knows our secret sins. *Proverbs 28:13*—When we hide our sins, we cannot prosper; we need to confess and forsake them to obtain God's mercy. *Ecclesiastes 12:14*—Every secret thing will be judged by God.

6. *Gideon*—He did it in obedience to God's instruction. *Hezekiah*—He did it because he wanted to follow the Lord and do what was right. *Josiah*—He sought to follow the Lord with his whole heart, soul, and might and to obey God's Word.

7. *Psalm 40:8*—We should delight in doing the will of God. *Psalm 42:1, 2*—Our souls should hunger and thirst after God. *Psalm 104:34*—We should find thinking about Him to be sweet; He makes us glad. *Colossians 3:1, 2*—We should set our affection on Christ and the things of God.

8. He was willing to put to death his dearly loved son because God told him to. His love and obedience to God were preeminent. (*Discuss:* What did Isaac represent to Abraham? What causes us to idolize people? How can Christ fill our lives more adequately than even people we love?)

9. *Moses*—His shepherd's rod. *The widow*—She gave what little meal and oil she had left. *The lad*—He gave his lunch.

10. (a) David wanted to build a house for worship of the Lord (a temple). (b) He asked who was willing to consecrate his service for the Lord. (c) They offered willingly what they had to the Lord's work. (d) David was humble, recognizing his and the people's unworthiness to serve God. (e) All that was given to do the work came from God. David didn't want the people to forget this (v. 18). (*Discuss:* How can we check our attitudes to be sure we are serving God for His glory and not for our own pride?)

11. *John 3:27*—The ability to do God's work is given from above. *John 15:5*—Any fruit we bear comes from Christ, and we can do nothing without Him. *Colossians 3:17*—Do all in Christ's name, giving thanks.

12. *Verse 7*—Submit yourself to God (see your need and come to God with it); resist the Devil (by submitting to God and drawing near to Him). *Verse 8*—Draw near to God (a continuing state); cleanse your hands (confess); purify your heart (hate sin; ask God for help with this). *Verse 9*—Mourn (be serious about sin in your life). *Verse 10*—Humble yourself (daily, moment-by-moment dependence upon Him).

13. Grace.

14. (a) They confessed their sin and burned their witchcraft books. (b) The Word of God prevailed in people's lives.

15. We are told to "put on the Lord Jesus Christ." We look to Him in faith to live His resurrection life through us (Gal. 2:20). As Christ becomes our daily focus, the desire to sin will abate.

16. Personal answers.

17. Christ paid for our redemption with His own blood.

Section III—1. Answers may include fear, loneliness, depression, discouragement, anger, guilt, insecurity.

2. Christ died for this sin; it is an awful thing. Sin no more has the right to rule over us (Rom. 6:14). God wants us to be purified from all sin (2 Cor. 7:1).

3. Refuse to yield yourself to sin (Rom. 6:12, 13). Find a specific verse that addresses the problem and meditate often on it. Pray for the Lord's enabling to overcome (Heb. 4:15, 16). Yield to the Holy Spirit's power (Rom. 8:12, 13).

4. You can't hide your sin from God. It affects your relationship with Him.

5. Personal answers.

6. Idolatry is sin! Therefore she must repent and put the idol away or give it over to God. She must desire to totally follow and obey her Lord. She must cultivate an ongoing goal of holiness so she will not fall back into idolatry. Through the Spirit's power she must exercise self-control and flee temptation. She should meditate on related verses and pray continually about this. When she "puts off" the idol, she must "put on" godly activities to fill the vacuum. She must recognize that this may be an ongoing battle, but the victory has already been assured for us by Christ!

7. We fear God will somehow take the person out of our lives. We fear having to do

without him or her. We may fear not being able to control that person. We may fear the loneliness that would result if we lost him or her. (*Discuss:* We often fear that God will allow a loved one to be killed. Where might these thoughts come from? What if God were to take a person from our lives? Is it wrong to strongly love a husband or child, for instance? What does Matthew 10:37 actually say?)

8. We worship God in spirit. If we are worshiping something else, we are not free to worship God as we should.

9. Personal answers.

10. Personal answers.

11. Personal answers.

LESSON 11

Section II—1. Prepare your heart by confessing sin; receive the Word with meekness; put it into practice; continue in it.

2. She deceives herself by hearing God's Word but not putting it into practice. (Such action deceives because we think of ourselves as being spiritual just because we've gone to church and heard the Word. The important thing to God is that we *do* His Word.) Also mentioned is forgetting the conviction of the Spirit and seeming to be religious.

3. Godly actions and words.

4. The sin in our flesh causes us to be deceitful. We can hardly comprehend the ways that sin affects the way we think and act.

5. Confess it and be cleansed.

6. We are saying God lies about us, and His Word is not dwelling in us.

7. Jesus Christ, Who sits at the Father's right hand. He intercedes for our cleansing by His sufficient sacrifice for every sin on the cross.

8. Obedience to God's commandments and His Word; the love of God maturing in our lives; growing to be more Christlike in all our ways.

9. *Proverbs 12:15*—Thinks she's right; won't listen to counsel (implied). *Matthew 7:3, 4*—Sees clearly the faults of others but not her own. *James 3:14-16*—Has bitter envy (the Greek word means "to desire to make war on the good it sees in others"); creates strife; is proud of it; justifies behavior with "earthly" arguments; creates confusion (her behavior disturbs the peace); does evil works.

10. *Genesis 3:1-13*—Adam blamed Eve; Eve blamed the serpent. *Genesis 4:3-9*—Cain lied and became defensive and sarcastic. *Exodus 32:1-6, 21-24*—Aaron justified his actions because of other people's sin; denied blame because things "just happened"; tried to spiritualize his sin (v. 5). (People may often offer "spiritual" reasons for their sins.) *1 Samuel 13:5-13*—Saul justified his sin by saying he had no choice but to do what he did. (We never *have* to do wrong.) He blamed circumstances.

11. *Proverbs 28:13*—She shall not prosper. *Proverbs 28:14*—She will fall into mischief. *John 15:4-6*—Spiritual unfruitfulness. *1 John 2:28*—Will be ashamed at Christ's return.

12. (a) God spoke to Israel through His Law, His Spirit, and the prophets. (b) God wanted Israel to show true judgment, mercy, compassion, concern for others, and godly thinking toward others. (c) Israel pulled away, wouldn't look God "in the eye," plugged up her ears, hardened her heart. (d) Stubbornness, pride.

13. *Proverbs 14:29*—Don't get angry; think about it. *Lamentations 3:39-42*—Don't complain but search your heart; examine your actions; repent and turn to God. *1 Corinthians 11:28-31*—Examine yourself; judge yourself so God won't have to chasten you. *Psalm 51:17*—Be broken and have genuine sorrow. *2 Corinthians 7:9, 10*—Have godly sorrow about your sin; such sorrow leads to repentance and deliverance.

14. (a) He felt old, tired out. God's hand was heavy upon him. Spiritually, he was "dried up." (b) He was joyful and blessed.

15. Well-behaved, meek, pure, peaceable, gentle, reasonable, merciful, full of good fruits, impartial (not prejudiced against certain people), without hypocrisy (not hiding anything), producing righteousness, sowing peace.

Section III—1. Answers include pride, self-protection, fear of exposure, stubbornness, enjoyment of sin.

2. God still speaks to us through His Word, His Spirit, and others who speak His Word to us. He may also use circumstances to chasten us, as He did with Israel.

3. Stop attending church or become sporadic in attendance; when attending, hear but don't "listen"; neglect personal prayer and Bible reading, or have these but keep it superficial; keep very busy to mask guilt and avoid God.

4. (a) Defensiveness usually indicates guilt and seeking to protect self. (b) Shifting the blame seeks to place the guilt on another. (c) Excuses are used to justify our actions. (d) Spiritualizing attempts to make our wrong seem right. (e) Harsh judgment of others is throwing up a smoke screen to draw attention away from our own sin.

5. Godly sorrow is genuine grief over your sin and offense against the holiness of God. Worldly sorrow is being sorry that your sin brought trouble on you. Paul says that godly sorrow leads to repentance, which is turning away from your sin and back to God.

6. A sinning Christian will continually battle the Holy Spirit's conviction. Though denying sin, the believer knows deep down inside she is grieving the Spirit and lacking the peace of God.

7. Acknowledgment of sin and guilt without justification of self; acceptance of consequences without bitterness; seeking God's cleansing and restoration. In some cases, asking forgiveness of others or making restitution may be necessary.

8. It discourages self-deceit and hardness of heart. It keeps us humble and brings our sin to the forefront of our minds so that we will continue to bring it before God. Confessing our faults to another makes us accountable so that others can check our spiritual progress or deterioration. Also, as the verse says, they can pray for us. (*Discuss:* How might the behavior of some Christians discourage others from revealing their struggles?)

9. Personal answers.

LESSON 12

Section II—1.*1 Corinthians 10:13*—God is faithful and will not allow us to be tempted above what we are able to bear. He will also provide a way of escape. *2 Corinthians 2:14*—God always causes us to triumph in Christ. *James 4:7*—If we submit to (put ourselves under) God's authority and resist Satan, he will flee from us.

2. He was tempted in every general area that we are tempted in, but He did not sin. If we come to Him for help against temptation, He will give us mercy and grace to help.

3. *Psalm 119:11*—God's Word being in our hearts and minds. *Matthew 26:41*—Being alert to temptation and praying that we will not give in. *Romans 6:12-14*—Having a yielded life. We recognize that we are no longer under sin's authority but God's. We now have His grace to overcome sin (see Titus 2:11, 12). *Galatians 5:16*—Moment by moment we must walk in (keep yielding to) the Spirit.

4. *Ephesians 6:16*—Faith is a shield to ward off attacks of Satan. *James 1:2-4*—When our faith is tested and strengthened, we develop spiritual endurance, which leads to maturity in Christ. *1 John 5:4, 5*—By our faith in Christ we have already overcome the world.

5. He was filled with the Holy Spirit's power. (We can be too.) He knew God's Word and how to use it against Satan's temptations. (We can too.) He could not be swayed from putting His total trust and dependence upon the Father for all His needs. By faith, He defeated Satan. (We can too!)

6. Hope, joy, peace in believing.

7. *1 Corinthians 1:30, 31*—Christ is your source of wisdom, righteousness, sanctification (growth in holiness), and redemption (deliverance). You need to glory in all that He is for you. *Philippians 3:7-10*—Knowing Christ surpasses all earthly gain. Everything else pales in comparison to knowing Him and being like Him. *Colossians 3:16, 17*—The Word of Christ must be entrenched in your heart and mind so that you can serve and worship Him. All your service is to be done unto Him. *1 Peter 2:21-25*—Christ is your example in suffering, in holiness, in submission, in sacrifice. He is your source of righteousness and comfort.

8. (a) He is merciful, faithful; He has suffered; He can help us. (b) Come boldly to God's throne to receive grace and mercy to help us.

9. He wants to be our first love.

10. *Matthew 22:37*—Fervently love God. *Hebrews 11:6*—Fervently seek Him. *Psalm 119:140, 162, 167*—Fervently love His Word. *1 Thessalonians 5:17*—Fervently pray. *Luke 6:35*—Fervently do good. *Psalm 100:2*—Fervently serve. *2 Corinthians 7:1*—Fervently seek holiness. *1 Peter 3:15*—Fervently witness.

11. (a) His desire was to accomplish God's will with each moment of His life. (b) Joy in His Spirit.

12. *2 Timothy 2:19-21*—We will depart from iniquity; we will be suitable for the Master's use and ready to work for Him. *Hebrews 10:23-25*—We will be steadfast in

the faith; we will encourage other believers; we will be regular in church attendance. *James 5:7, 8*—We will patiently wait for God to work out His purposes; we will be mindful of Christ's return.

13. The joy of finishing well.

14. *1 Corinthians 15:57, 58*—God always gives us the victory, so we should be steadfast and continue to work for Him. Our work for Him is never wasted. *Philippians 1:6*—As we endeavor to be faithful to Him, He is faithfully working in us. *1 Thessalonians 5:23, 24*—God is faithful to sanctify us and keep us until redemption.

15. Nothing can separate us from the love that Christ has for us, and through Him we are more than conquerors.

Section III—1. Freedom from sin brings joy through a clear conscience (guilt removed); decrease of conflicts and problems; knowing we are pleasing God.

2. Reasons often include busyness; too many distractions (kids, phone); too difficult to understand; don't know where to begin. (*Discuss:* What are the solutions to these supposed problems?)

3. Ideas include read; study; memorize Scripture; go to Sunday School, church, Bible study; read books that teach Scripture; attend conferences; listen to tapes, radio (but make sure all these are sound and Biblical in their presentation).

4. You can ask Him to increase your faith; attend church regularly; read the Word (Psalms is an excellent book for growing in a knowledge of God's character); keep a record of answers to prayer; write in a journal what God is doing in your life; talk to others about what God is doing in their lives; read biographies of great and godly Christians.

5. Post a verse and stop a moment to study and reflect upon it. Take a moment for a "prayer break"—at meals or when the Lord puts something on your heart. Use the beauty of creation to quiet your heart for a moment and reflect upon the greatness of the Creator. Spend a moment telling someone of a blessing of your day.

6. We really must step back and evaluate our lives. If we truly have no time to quiet ourselves before God, we should eliminate activities. Let God direct us into the areas of service He wants us to do. Learn to say no. Spiritual fervency requires a balanced life physically and mentally and time to communicate with God. Remember Mary!

7. Personal answers.

8. Personal answers.

9. Personal answers.